Everything for Fall

A COLLECTION FROM GRYPHON HOUSE BOOKS

Everything for Fall

A Complete Activity Book for Teachers of Young Children

Edited by Kathy Charner
Illustrations by Joan Waites

ACTIVITIES FOR SEPTEMBER, OCTOBER AND NOVEMBER

gryphon house
Beltsville, Maryland

Copyright © 1997 Gryphon House, Inc.
Published by Gryphon House, Inc.
10726 Tucker Street, Beltsville, MD 20705

World Wide Web: http://www.ghbooks. com

Text Illustrations: Joan Waites

Library of Congress Cataloging-in-Publication Data

Everything for fall : a complete activity book for teachers of young
    children : activities for September, October, and November / edited
    by Kathy Charner.
        p.   cm.
    "A collection from Gryphon House books."
    Includes bibliographical references and index.
    ISBN 0-87659-185-3 (pbk.)
    1. Early childhood education--Activity programs.   2. Autumn.
I. Charner, Kathy.
LB1139.35.A37E84   1997
372.21--DC21   97-21503
                                                              CIP

Fall
Table of Contents

November

Introduction

Ever wish you could have the advice and suggestions of early childhood experts at your fingertips? It's in this book. With expertise in language, science, math, art, circle and group time, music, transitions and much more, this book gives you just what you need when you need it, in an easy-to-use format. This book contains activities, ideas and suggestions from the following time-tested books:

500 Five Minute Games
Earthways
Hug a Tree
More Mudpies to Magnets
More Story S-t-r-e-t-c-h-e-r-s
Mudpies to Magnets
One Potato, Two Potato, Three Potato, Four
Preschool Art
Story S-t-r-e-t-c-h-e-r-s
The Complete Learning Center Book
The Giant Encyclopedia of Circle Time and Group Activities
The Giant Encyclopedia of Theme Activities for Children 2 to 5
The Instant Curriculum
The Learning Circle
The Outside Play and Learning Book
The Peaceful Classroom
ThemeStorming
Transition Time
Where Is Thumbkin?

Activities appropriate for children

This book is chock-full of activities that teachers have used successfully with children for years. Teachers enjoy the activities because they are appropriate for children and because they are easy to do. Children enjoy the activities because they are fun and filled with things to learn. Whether you teach younger children or older children, or children who have difficulty understanding science concepts or those who need just a little extra help mastering language skills, there is something for you in this book.

A complete plan

Use this book to plan a morning, a day, a week, a month of activities, a whole season, or, with all three books, a whole school year. There are both teacher-directed and child-directed activities in the book. So while most of the children are independently exploring activities, the teacher can work with one or a few children who have expressed an interest in a certain area or who need additional work in a specific area.

A monthly plan

As written, this book offers teachers a complete plan for three months. Use this book to develop a monthly plan for September, October and November, using the variety of activities presented, or open the book to any page when you need an activity to fill a morning, a few hours or just a few minutes. This book offers both possibilities. The short sentence or paragraph that introduces each activity often contains learning objectives, an additional help to teachers for planning.

Integrated curriculum

Although the activities are drawn from different books, most of the activities in each month are related to certain topics or themes, the thematic threads of each month. Other activities related to the season or month (or because they were too much fun to leave out of the book) are also included in each chapter.

The thematic threads for September are:
>   Back to School
>   Apples
>   Leaves

The thematic threads for October are:
>   Farms
>   Falling Leaves
>   Halloween

The thematic threads for November are:
>   Homes and Houses
>   Families and Feelings
>   Thanksgiving

Create your own integrated curriculum that meets the needs and interests of your children by selecting related activities for one day, such as circle time, art and math activities, or plan a whole week of activities about Apples (or Farms or Homes and Houses or any other thematic thread) that includes activities from all areas of the curriculum.

The monthly chapters

This book has three chapters; each chapter is a complete month of activities containing the following:

Fingerplays, songs and poems—use them during circle time or enjoy them anytime during the day.

Ideas and suggestions for 2 learning centers—learning centers are great child-oriented places where children experiment, create and learn about their world.

Art activities—children love to express their thoughts, feelings, accomplishments and discoveries through art. The activities focus on the process of art, not the product.

Circle time and group activities—activities for the times when all your wonderful individual children are learning to be part of a larger group. These activities, as with most of the activities in the book, are related to the month or the thematic threads of the month.

Dramatic play activities—children need little encouragement in this area. Just set up these activities, and let the children play!

Language activities—language acquisition, prereading skills and expressive language are just a few of the language skills children learn with these activities.

Math activities—activities that are fun, easy-to-do and appropriate for young children. The activities build a conceptual base to help children understand beginning math concepts.

Music and movement activities—children love to sing and move. Activities include old favorites and suggestions to turn old favorites into new favorites. Additionally, unique activities to encourage children to get up, move around and learn what their bodies can do are included in this section.

Science activities—filled with hands-on activities to help children begin to answer the many "why" questions and learn science skills of estimation, scientific method, problem solving, cause and effect relationships and lots more.

Snack and cooking activities—children love cooking projects—experimenting with ingredients, then proudly serving the result to the other children. Activities range from simple recipes with a few ingredients to those requiring more time and ingredients. Children will love them all!

Transition activities—ever wonder how to get a child who is engrossed in sand play ready for snack? Or clean up before circle time? Or get a group of children to come inside after outdoor play? Or to settle down to hear a story? This section is filled with tried-and-true activities.

Games—enjoy a fun time with a few children or the whole group. Play a game to help children learn math skills, coordination, language skills, listening skills, kindness or cooperation.

Suggested books—filled with books children and teachers love that are related to the season or the thematic threads of the month.

Recommended records and tapes—filled with records or tapes of songs that children and teachers love and that are related to the season or the thematic threads of the month.

The activities in each chapter

The activities in each chapter (month) contain the following:

Title of activity and suggested age—The title and suggested age tell what the activity is about and the ages most likely to enjoy and learn from the activity.
Note: Individual teachers are the best judges of children in their care. The ages are meant as a suggestion only.

Short introduction—This short sentence or paragraph describes the activity, suggests a learning objective or a combination of both.

Words to use—Language skills and vocabulary acquisition are developing rapidly in young children. Use this list of words while doing the activity, when talking about what the children will do or when discussing the activity after completion. The words range from simple to complex. Individual teachers will know best which words to introduce and use with their children.

Materials—A list of all the materials needed for the activity.

What to do—A step-by-step description of each activity. Helpful hints are often included as well as any cautionary notes necessary.

Want to do more?—This section includes suggestions for extending the activity using different materials or expanding it into other areas of the curriculum. For example, an art activity might suggest a different material to use instead of paper, or a circle time activity might suggest a related science or math activity.

Teaching tips—This section may include specific ways to help children with the activity. For example, a suggestion to tape the paper to the table so it does not move while the child is drawing. Or it may contain suggestions to make the activity simpler for younger children or more complex for older ones. Additionally, this section also may include general tips about working with children such as helping children learn respect for others, reminding teachers that young children get over-stimulated easily and other tips of that nature.

Home connections—The connection of home and school is a critical one. Teachers are often looking for ways to help parents feel more connected with what goes on in school. This section contains suggestions of how an activity can be done at home with parents, which may help parents feel more connected to the school or child care facility and help them understand what their child does during the day.

Books to read and records and tapes—Suggestions of books, records and tapes that relate to the activity.

SEPTEMBER *fall*

Fingerplays, Poems and Songs

Hickory, Dickory, Dock

Hickory, dickory, dock.
The mouse ran up the clock.
The clock struck one,
The mouse ran down.
Hickory, dickory, dock.

★ ONE POTATO, TWO POTATO, THREE POTATO, FOUR

One, Two, Buckle My Shoe

One, two, buckle my shoe
Three, four, shut the door
Five, six, pick up sticks
Seven, eight, lay them straight
Nine, ten, a good fat hen
Eleven, twelve, dig and delve
Thirteen, fourteen, maids a-courting
Fifteen, sixteen, maids a-milking
Seventeen, eighteen, maids a-waiting
Nineteen, twenty, my plate is empty.

★ ONE POTATO, TWO POTATO, THREE POTATO, FOUR

Jack Be Nimble

Jack be nimble, Jack be quick,
Jack jump over the candlestick.

★ ONE POTATO, TWO POTATO, THREE POTATO, FOUR

Little Miss Muffet

Little Miss Muffet sat on her tuffet,
Eating her curds and whey;
Along came a spider and sat down beside her
And frightened Miss Muffet away.

★ ONE POTATO, TWO POTATO, THREE POTATO, FOUR

Way Up High in the Apple Tree

Way up high (point up)
In the apple tree.
Two little apples (hold up two fingers)
Smiled down at me. (look down and smile)
I shook that tree (pretend to shake a tree)
As hard as I could.
And down came the apples. (bring apples down)
MMMM! MMMM! GOOD! (pat tummy)

★ TRANSITION TIME

Open, Shut Them

Open, shut them, open, shut them,
Give a little clap.
Open, shut them, open, shut them,
Put them in your lap.

Creep them, creep them, creep them, creep
   them,
Right up to your chin.
Open wide your smiling mouth,
But do not let them in.

Creep them, creep them, creep them, creep
   them,
Past your cheeks and chin.
Open wide your smiling eyes,
Peeking in—BOO.

Creep them, creep them, creep them, creep
   them,
Right down to your toes.
Let them fly up in the air and,
Bop you on the nose.

Open, shut them, open, shut them,
Give a little clap.
Open, shut them, open, shut them,
Put them in your lap.

★ WHERE IS THUMBKIN?

Head, Shoulders, Knees and Toes

Head, shoulders, knees and toes, knees and toes,
Head, shoulders, knees and toes, knees and toes,
And eyes and ears and mouth and nose.
Head, shoulders, knees and toes, knees and toes.

★ WHERE IS THUMBKIN?

Hokey Pokey

You put your right hand in,
You put your right hand out,
You put your right hand in
And you shake it all about.
You do the hokey pokey,
And you turn yourself around,
That's what it's all about.

You put your left hand in....
You put your right foot in....
You put your left foot in....
You put your right elbow in....
You put your left elbow in....
You put your backside in....
You put your head in....
You put your whole self in....

★ WHERE IS THUMBKIN?

If You're Happy and You Know It

If you're happy and you know it, clap your
   hands. (clap, clap)
If you're happy and you know it, clap your
   hands. (clap, clap)
If you're happy and you know it, then your life
   will surely show it.
If you're happy and you know it, clap your
   hands. (clap, clap)

If you're happy and you know it, stomp your
   feet (stomp, stomp)....

If you're happy and you know it, shout,
   "Hooray!" (shout "hooray")....

★ WHERE IS THUMBKIN?

September Learning Centers

Housekeeping Center

While playing in the Housekeeping Center children learn:

1. To expand their language skills as they talk about the activities taking place.
2. To become confident of their capabilities as they dramatize familiar happenings.
3. To begin to understand other people and learn about their needs and responsibilities.

Suggested Props for the Housekeeping Center

kitchen appliances (can be made out of cardboard boxes)

stove	refrigerator
sink	

small table with chairs

baby doll, baby bed, high chair, bottles

sink with cabinet for washing and storing
   dishes

cleaning tools and materials such as

sponges	vacuum cleaner
broom and dust pan	mop and bucket

collection of empty containers such as

cereal boxes	cans of soup
boxes of pasta	laundry detergent
frozen vegetables	spices

cooking utensils such as

pots	pans
skillets	rolling pin
cookie sheet	muffin pan
egg beater	

communication tools such as
   telephone
   radio
   intercom/walkie talkie

full length unbreakable mirror

collection of dress-up clothes (Add items that are appropriate to wear during the season such as heavy coats, hats, mittens and boots during winter. Clothing should also be available for different ages and sizes, including baby clothes, clothes for adults and older persons. Both male and female clothing should be in the Housekeeping Center.)

Curriculum Connections

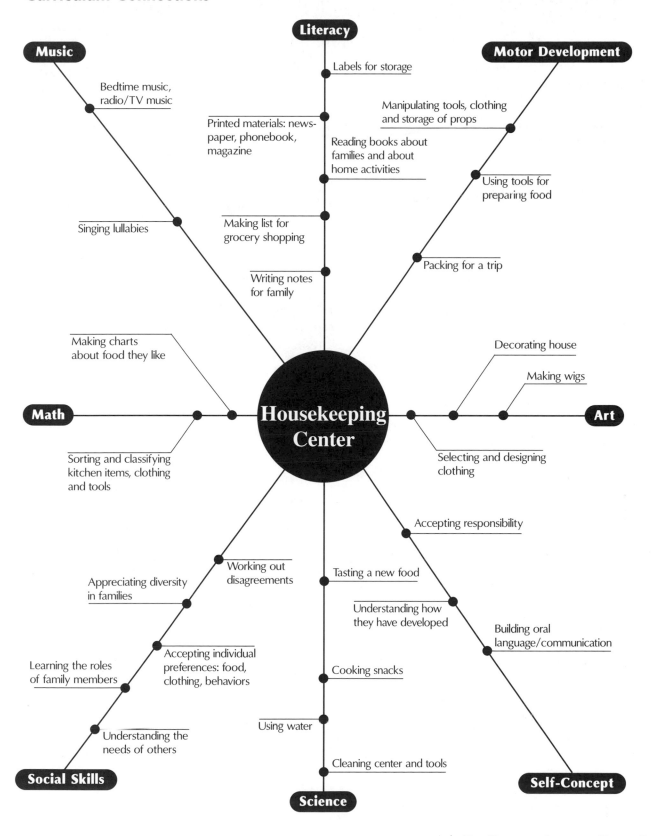

Music
- Bedtime music, radio/TV music
- Singing lullabies

Literacy
- Labels for storage
- Printed materials: newspaper, phonebook, magazine
- Reading books about families and about home activities
- Making list for grocery shopping
- Writing notes for family

Motor Development
- Manipulating tools, clothing and storage of props
- Using tools for preparing food
- Packing for a trip

Math
- Making charts about food they like
- Sorting and classifying kitchen items, clothing and tools

Art
- Decorating house
- Making wigs
- Selecting and designing clothing

Housekeeping Center

Social Skills
- Working out disagreements
- Appreciating diversity in families
- Accepting individual preferences: food, clothing, behaviors
- Learning the roles of family members
- Understanding the needs of others

Science
- Tasting a new food
- Cooking snacks
- Using water
- Cleaning center and tools

Self-Concept
- Accepting responsibility
- Understanding how they have developed
- Building oral language/communication

★ THE COMPLETE LEARNING CENTER BOOK

Art Center

While playing in the Art Center children learn:

1. To become more creative.
2. To understand their world as they experiment with many different materials and tools.
3. To learn about artists and illustrators.
4. To build their self-confidence as they make decisions and implement ideas.

Suggested Props for the Art Center

easel
water source (sink or tub of water)
paintbrushes
markers
chalk
crayons
paint rollers
sponges
scissors
glue
feathers
clay
playdough (made from different recipes)
three-dimensional materials such as

pie plates	small boxes
pipe cleaners	straws
electrical wire pieces	bubble wrap
cotton	toothpicks

different kinds of paper such as

manila	construction
newsprint	fingerpaint
wallpaper	foil
tissue paper	paper towels
coffee filters	newspapers
wax paper	computer paper
cardboard	

colored paper (in a variety of colors, sizes and textures)
painting smocks or old shirts
large sheets of plastic, newspaper or shower curtain liners (to cover tables and floor)

Curriculum Connections

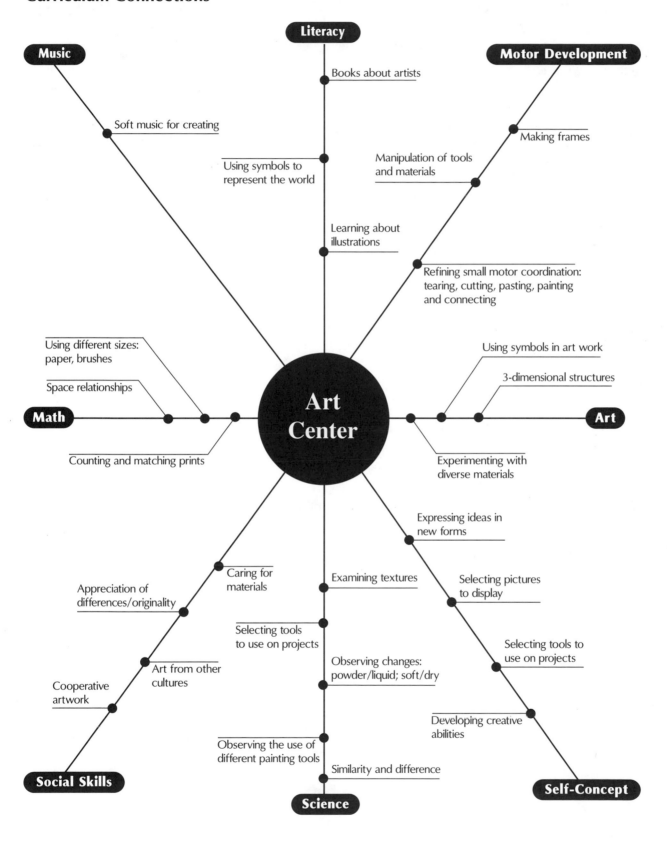

Music

Soft music for creating

Literacy

Books about artists

Using symbols to represent the world

Learning about illustrations

Motor Development

Making frames

Manipulation of tools and materials

Refining small motor coordination: tearing, cutting, pasting, painting and connecting

Math

Using different sizes: paper, brushes

Space relationships

Counting and matching prints

Art Center

Using symbols in art work

3-dimensional structures

Art

Experimenting with diverse materials

Expressing ideas in new forms

Social Skills

Appreciation of differences/originality

Cooperative artwork

Caring for materials

Art from other cultures

Examining textures

Selecting tools to use on projects

Observing changes: powder/liquid; soft/dry

Observing the use of different painting tools

Similarity and difference

Science

Selecting pictures to display

Selecting tools to use on projects

Developing creative abilities

Self-Concept

★ THE COMPLETE LEARNING CENTER BOOK

Art Activities

Pick an Apple—To Learn Your Name

3+

Teaches children how to recognize their names.

Words to use

tree
trunk
apple
tape

Materials

green, brown and red poster board
scissors
small box, basket, pail or crate
marker
contact paper or laminating film, optional
masking tape

What to do

1. Cut out a green tree-top and brown trunk from the poster board. Cut a red apple for each child. Make sure the tree is big enough to place an apple for each child. Laminate the tree.
2. Write a child's name on each apple. Laminate each apple or cover with contact paper, if desired.
3. Place the tree on a wall or door low enough for children to reach.
4. Put apples on the tree with masking tape rolled sticky side out.
5. Call a child's name and let the child pick his name apple and put it in a container placed nearby.

Want to do more?

This could be used for surnames, numbers, letters of the alphabet, etc.

★ THE GIANT ENCYCLOPEDIA OF THEME ACTIVITIES

Nature Collage

An exciting, interesting way to learn about the properties of natural items.

Words to use

collage
glue
wood
stick
nature
dry

Materials

white glue
Styrofoam grocery tray
nature items such as pebbles, bark,
   leaves, nuts, pine needles, pine
   cones, seeds, wood shavings,
   shells, seed pods or dried weeds
piece of wood for base
craft stick or cotton swab

What to do

1. Squeeze a puddle of glue in the
   middle of a Styrofoam grocery
   tray.
2. Select an item from nature and arrange it on the base piece of wood. Dab the item with glue from
   a craft stick or cotton swab. The artist may also choose to dip the item in the puddle of glue.
3. Now stick the item on the base piece of wood.
4. Add more bits of things from nature and attach them to the piece of wood with glue.
5. When satisfied with the arrangement, allow the collage to dry overnight or for several days.

Want to do more?

Using a felt pen or paint, color the wood base and then glue the nature items into the color design.
A Nature Collage can be made on fabric-covered wood, a paper plate, cardboard, plaster of Paris in a
pie plate or any number of other backgrounds.

Teaching tips

As an alternative to white glue, a glue gun provides immediate, strong, long-lasting results. Constant
one-on-one adult supervision is necessary when using a glue gun.

★ PRESCHOOL ART

Fingerpaint Leaves

3+

Encourages the development of small motor skills.

Words to use

fingerpaint
smear
smooth
print

Materials

big, soft fall leaves
fingerpaint in containers
big paper or newsprint
newspaper-covered work
   surface
soapy water in bucket for clean-
   up
towel

What to do

1. Collect big, soft fall leaves (such as maple leaves) that are still supple.
2. Place a leaf on the newspaper.
3. Dip fingers in the fingerpaint and smooth and smear paint all over one side of the leaf.
4. Use fingers to draw designs into the paint on the leaf.
5. Wash and dry hands.
6. Place a sheet of newsprint over the leaf and, with gentle pressure, pat the paper onto the painted leaf.
7. Peel the paper away from the leaf or peel the leaf off of the paper.
8. An imprint from the fingerpainting and the leaf will be transferred to the paper.

Teaching tips

A simple fingerpaint recipe is to mix a quarter cup of liquid starch and a tablespoon of powdered or liquid tempera paint. Stir with a stick and use as fingerpaint. The measurements are not strict so experiment with color, intensity and thickness.

★ PRESCHOOL ART

Grocery Sack Leaves

3+

Teaches small motor skills while children enjoy this painting and cutting activity.

Words to use

square   red
yellow   brown
green   trace
cut

Materials

scissors   brown grocery sacks (bags)
dry tempera paint   paintbrushes
pencils or markers

What to do

1. Provide each child with a large square cut from a brown grocery sack.
2. Display a fall leaf and discuss the variety of colors.
3. Sprinkle several colors of dry tempera paint on the sack squares (red, yellow, brown, green, etc.)
4. Let the children mix the colors by painting with water and a brush.
5. When dry, place a leaf pattern on the painted paper. The children trace around the pattern and cut it out.

Want to do more?

The leaves can be used for a fall bulletin board, or children can take them home.

★ THE INSTANT CURRICULUM

Tissue Square Leaves

4+

Teaches about changing leaf colors, differences in shapes and names of leaves (oak, elm, maple).

Words to use

oak   maple
elm   leaf

Materials

precut poster board oak, elm and maple leaves (about 7" x 10")
tissue squares in fall colors, 1" wide
white glue thinned with water
brushes and containers for glue
newspaper
crayons
scissors

What to do

1. Precut leaf shapes, cutting enough to allow each child a choice. Cover tables with newspaper for painting and drying. Precut 1 inch tissue squares in fall colors. Thin glue and pour into containers.
2. Each child chooses a leaf and writes his name on it.
3. The children cover half the leaf surface with glue mixture and then apply squares to the glue-covered half, overlapping the edges. Repeat with the second half of leaf.
4. Spread glue over the entire surface to seal tissue squares. Allow to dry. Trim off excess tissue to show shape of leaf.

Want to do more?

Go on a fall walk to collect leaves and objects. Use tissue leaves to chart, graph and classify on the rug or bulletin board.

Book to read

A Tree Is Nice by Janice Udry

★ GIANT ENCYCLOPEDIA OF THEME ACTIVITIES

Textured Hands and Feet   4+

Teaches children about the shape and size of their hands and feet.

Words to use

hands
feet
trace
cut

Materials

textured paper (wallpaper samples)
markers
scissors

What to do

1. The children trace around their hands and feet on textured paper (wallpaper is great!).
2. Cut them out. Younger children may need help cutting out their hands and feet.
3. Use for bulletin boards or to create a mural or collage.

★ WHERE IS THUMBKIN?

Chalky Leaf Spatter

What a fun (and maybe a bit messy) way to practice small motor skills.

Words to use

tape
screen
frame
chalk

Materials

nail brush
wire screen, stapled to old
    picture frame
thin tempera paint in a bowl
chalk
paper
pressed leaves, flowers or any flat items
large cardboard box with one side cut out
tape
smock or old shirt

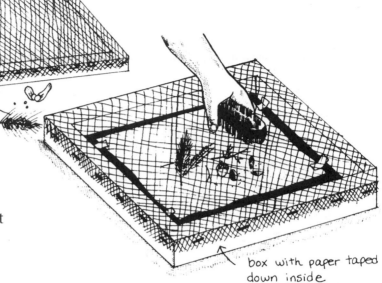

wire screen
stapled over picture frame

box with paper taped
down inside

What to do

1. Place a sheet of paper inside the box and tape the edges down so it won't wiggle.
2. Place leaves, flowers, grasses or paper shapes on the paper.
3. Place the wire screen in the frame over the paper. The screen should be several inches above the paper.
4. Dip the nail brush into the paint.
5. Rub the paint-filled brush many times across the screen. If the brush is loaded with paint, the spatter drops will be big and coarse.
6. Next take a piece of chalk and rub it across the screen. Bits of chalk will fall through the screen and land in the wet paint adding additional color to the spatter design. If the screen gets clogged with paint, rinse it clean, shake it dry and then add the chalk.
7. Dry the completed artwork. Remove the leaves and other objects or stencils.

Teaching tips

The box keeps the splattering paint within a boundary. Be sure to cover the child with an old shirt too.

★ PRESCHOOL ART

Finger Puppets

5+

Develops the imagination; encourages storytelling.

Words to use

finger

stitch

story

zigzag

imagination

Materials

felt pieces, about 3" x 2"

sewing machine

fabric scraps, buttons, sequins, feathers and craft eyes

white glue or hobby glue

felt pens

scissors

What to do

1. With adult help cut two pieces of felt, about 3 inches long by 2 inches wide.
2. Place one piece of felt on top of the other and sew a zigzag stitch around the felt, making the top rounded and leaving the bottom open for finger access.
3. Have the artist glue any materials to the base to create an animal, person or character. Use felt pens to add features. Let the puppet dry.
4. Make up stories, plays or dances using the finger puppets as the main characters.

stitch

GLUE

Want to do more?

Cut the fingers off an old glove and make each glove segment a puppet. Make puppet characters from a favorite book and act out the story with the puppets. Sing a song with the finger puppets.

Teaching tips

Some young artists may be able to sew the base together with supervision. Measurements can be adjusted for size.

★ Preschool Art

Branch Weaving

Teaches about the properties of natural materials.

Words to use

branch   weave
wrap   wool
strips

Materials

tree branch with at least three
    smaller branches shooting out
yarn in many colors and textures
wool
nature items such as long grasses,
    weeds, feathers or corn husks
strips of fabric, ribbon and other
    strings or cords
scissors

What to do

1. With adult help, start at the top
   or the bottom of one small
   branch by looping some yarn
   around the branch to get the
   project started.
2. Wrap yarn around smaller
   branches to make a base of yarn
   moving up or down the branches like a spider web.
3. Weave other yarn, wool, grasses, fabric strips or any intriguing items into the yarn base. Random
   weaving and wrapping is also effective.
4. Wrap and weave until the branch weaving is complete.

Want to do more?

Nail or glue strips of thin wood into a frame or box shape. Wrap and weave yarns on the wood base.

Teaching tips

Keep the yarn about two feet in length so it doesn't get out of control. When the yarn is too short it
can be frustrating and when it is too long it gets tangled. More yarn can always be added as each
piece is used up.

★ PRESCHOOL ART

Circle Time and Group Activities

All About Our Day   3+

Encourages children to think and talk about daily activities and routines, and works on sequencing.

Words to use

first
next
last

Materials

magazines, catalogs   scissors
construction paper   tape or glue
markers

What to do

1. In advance, cut pieces from magazines and catalogs representing the daily sequence of activities. Mount the pictures on construction paper and label the pictures with the activity, such as Arrival, Play Time, Snack.
2. At circle time show the children the pictures and talk about what happens in the classroom during that time of the day.
3. Talk about the daily schedule and ask the children to place the pictures in sequence according to the schedule.

★ GIANT ENCYCLOPEDIA OF CIRCLE TIME AND GROUP ACTIVITIES

Get Acquainted Song   3+

Helps children learn how to meet new friends and learn about people; incorporates the concepts of names and identity.

Words to use

acquaint   meet
greet   name
self   friends
sing

Materials

What to do

1. At circle time ask the children what it means to get acquainted with someone. Talk about their responses.
2. Tell the children that you will teach them the "Get Acquainted Song." Tell them what to do during the song (point to each child in turn who will stand up and say her name). Explain that after everyone says their names (including the teacher) then all the children will say their names at the same time.
3. Sing the following song to the tune of "Alouette."

> *Gather 'round it's time to get acquainted.*
> *Sing this song, and I'll show you how it's done.*
> *All you do to play this game*
> *Is stand right up and say your name. (child says name and everyone repeats*
> *the child's name)*
> *Ohhh! (Repeat the song with the children and teacher taking turns saying their*
> *names. After singing the song for the last time, all the children say their*
> *names together at the same time.)*

Want to do more?

Language: Use a drum or other percussion instrument when the children say their names. Beat the drum for each syllable in the name. Ask the children to stand up if their name has one drum beat (syllable). Repeat saying the names of the children whose names have one syllable. Continue saying the names of children whose names have two drum beats, three drum beats and four drum beats. After saying the children's names and beating the drum the number of times corresponding with the number of syllables in their names, allow the children to take turns playing their names on the drum when singing the song.

Social studies: Sing the "Get Acquainted Song" to introduce community helpers.

★ GIANT ENCYCLOPEDIA OF CIRCLE TIME AND GROUP ACTIVITIES

Roll That Ball   3+

Helps children learn the names of everyone in the group.

Words to use

name	roll
one at a time	ball

Materials

large ball

What to do

1. At circle time explain that you will roll a ball to one child and that child will say his name and then roll the ball to another child (only the child who has the ball may talk).
2. This activity can be varied using a different topic to learn more about the children (favorite foods, colors, toys, pets). After the children say their names, they respond to a topic, for example, "My name is Raoul and my favorite food is pizza."

Book to read

My Teacher Sleeps in School by Leatie Weiss

Song to sing

"What Is Your Name?" by Hap Palmer

★ GIANT ENCYCLOPEDIA OF CIRCLE TIME AND GROUP ACTIVITIES

Autumn Breezes
3+

Teaches about the wind.

Words to use

breeze   wind
push   lift
blow   feather

Materials

construction paper
scissors
feathers

What to do

1. Cut each sheet of paper in half.
2. At circle time discuss autumn breezes.
3. Spark interest with questions such as: How does a breeze feel? How does the wind feel? If you were an autumn breeze, what would you like to push, lift or blow against?
4. After the breeze discussion, each child chooses a feather and a sheet of construction paper.
5. The children fold their papers in half.
6. They stand up, drop their feathers and create a breeze by waving their papers. Who can keep the feather up?

Want to do more?

Drop a variety of objects and observe how a gentle breeze effects each one. Drop a leaf, a cotton ball, a balloon, a tissue, a paper cup and a crunched up piece of paper. Which one falls the quickest? Use a fan to create a wind. Drop the same objects in front of the fan and watch what happens.

Home connection

Tell the children that when they complete this activity they may choose one of the objects to take home with their folded papers. Then they can share this experience at home.

★ THE LEARNING CIRCLE

Create a Class Tree   3+

Teaches how to observe seasonal changes.

Words to use

fall
change
weather
sounds
hear
colors
see
textures
feel

Materials

small brown lunch bags
crayons
tape
white paper
large sheet of brown paper

What to do

1. Gather the children at the circle time area. Introduce the season of fall. Talk about the changes that fall brings (cool weather, leaves changing colors and falling, school starting).
2. Take the children for a nature walk. Give each child a small brown lunch bag. Have the children collect leaves of various kinds, colors and sizes. Point out textures, colors, sights and sounds of the season.
3. Back in the classroom, ask children to sort the leaves by color.
4. Ask each child to select two or three leaves to use in making rubbings. The child places the leaf under a piece of white paper and rubs the paper with a crayon.
5. The leaves are cut out and taped to a paper outline of a tree to create a class tree.

Want to do more?

Creative movement: Play flowing music and have children move like leaves blowing in the wind.
Math: Graph the leaves by color.
Science: Examine leaves with a magnifying glass.

Books to read

Autumn by Gerda Muller
Why Do Leaves Change Color by Betsy Maestro

★ Giant Encyclopedia of Circle Time and Group Activities

Fall Leaves   3+

Teaches about different leaf patterns and colors.

Words to use

leaf	color
size	most
least	

Materials

different leaf patterns cut out of different colors of construction paper (scattered around the room)

What to do

1. Ask each child to find a leaf in the room and bring it to circle time.
2. Once the children are sitting in the circle, ask them about their leaf. Ask who found leaves that look the same.
3. Sort out the leaves first by size. Count and see which group has the most and which group has the least.
4. Then sort the leaves by colors. Count the leaves again and see which group has more and which has less or the same number.
5. The children each hold a leaf, stand up pretending to be a tree and let the leaves fall to the ground. After the children pick up their leaves, ask them to drop only the yellow leaves, then the red leaves, then the green leaves, then the brown leaves.

Want to do more?

Outdoors: Have circle time outside and watch the leaves falling. Go leaf hunting. Collect the leaves to sort or use for collages. Rake the leaves on the playground and jump in them.
Sensory: Put a collection of leaves into a tub and let children explore them with magnifying glasses.

Books to read

A Busy Year by Leo Lionni
Caps, Hats, Socks and Mittens by Louise Borden

★ The Giant Encyclopedia of Circle Time and Group Activities

Leaf People

Teaches about the colors of leaves and how they fall from trees.

Words to use

yellow   orange
green   brown
red   fall
leaf   blow
wind

Materials

paper bag
colored leaves
scarves

What to do

1. At circle time ask the children to guess what is in the bag.
2. Pull out different color leaves from the bag and ask the children to name the colors.
3. Ask the children what color they would like to be if they were a leaf. Children discuss their choices.
4. Pretend to be leaves in a bag. Count to three and let's turn ourselves into leaves (1-2-3).
5. Now let's jump out of the bag (1-2-3).
6. Pretend we are big trees (extend arms). Let's grow leaves on the tree (shake hands).
7. Pretend to be the wind. The wind blows the leaves to the ground. (The teacher is the wind and the children, the "leaves," gently fall to the ground).
8. Now the children stand up and raise their hands above their heads. Then they make their hands fall, touching the ground. The teacher asks the children to copy her motions of raising and lowering her arms as she walks around the room. The teacher leads the children in the following chant.

> *Yellow leaves falling down*
> *Orange leaves falling down*
> *Green leaves falling down*
> *Brown leaves falling down*
> *Red leaves falling down*
> *Falling to the ground, falling to the ground. (children gently fall to the ground)*

★ GIANT ENCYCLOPEDIA OF CIRCLE TIME AND GROUP ACTIVITIES

Making Imaginary Applesauce

3+

Once you have had the experience of making real applesauce with your children, make it again—but let the children be the apples!

Words to use

apple
applesauce
cook
cinnamon

Materials

masking tape, optional

What to do

1. Make a large circle on the floor with the masking tape. This will be your cooking pot. Have the children sit in a circle around the pot.

2. Walk around the outside of the circle singing the first verse of the song and each time you sing "cut," touch a child on the shoulder. These children become the apple pieces and go into the pot and take a seat. Continue until all the children (apple pieces!) are in the pot with no core, seeds or stems.

"Applesauce Song" (to the tune of "The Mulberry Bush")

This is the way I cut the apples, cut the apples, cut the apples,
This is the way I cut the apples,
Making applesauce.

Now I'll pour the water on, the water on, the water on,
Now I'll pour the water on, (pretend to pour water on the children)
Making applesauce.

This is the way the apples cook, the apples cook, the apples cook,
This is the way the apples cook, (pretend to stir the children)
Making applesauce.

Now I'll stir the cinnamon in, etc. ... (pretend to sprinkle cinnamon on
*   the children)*
Now I'll stir the apples 'round, etc. ... (pretend to stir the children)

Now it's cooked and it can cool, it can cool, it can cool,
Now it's cooked and it can cool,
I've made my applesauce. (Sing this verse quietly.)

3. As you sing the Applesauce Song, add the ingredients one by one and stir the apples using a very large (imaginary) spoon! Have the children act out each part, boiling and bubbling in the beginning and becoming mushy by the end.
4. When the song is done, tell the children to be very still while the applesauce is cooling. Taste your delicious children!

Want to do more?

Make and enjoy real applesauce for snack.

★ THE GIANT ENCYCLOPEDIA OF THEME ACTIVITIES

From Seed to Pear   3+

Teaches about how pears grow and ripen.

Words to use

seed   tree
grow   pear
blossom   green
yellow   ripe

Materials

From Seed to Pear by Ali Mitgutsch
green pears and ripe pears
knife and cutting board

What to do

1. Cut a large juicy pear down the middle and show the children the seeds.
2. Ask them how long they think it will take for the seed to grow into a tree.
3. Read *From Seed to Pear*. Pause and emphasize the illustrations of the white blossoms turning into little hard green pears and then into ripe juicy yellow ones. If possible, show a green pear from the grocery and one which is ripened.
4. Cut some green pears and some ripe pears into small bite-sized pieces. Have the children taste them and compare the tastes and textures.
5. Place the *From Seed to Pear* book in the science and nature center for future reference.

★ STORY S-T-R-E-T-C-H-E-R-S

"Who's Missing?"

4+

Develops observation skills.

Words to use

missing
cover
blanket

Materials

blanket

What to do

1. At circle time explain that the children will play "Who's Missing?" Ask the children to sit on the floor and cover their eyes.
2. Cover one child with a blanket.
3. Tell the children to open their eyes and look around to see who is missing.
4. Children guess until they discover who is missing. The missing child takes the next turn covering another child with the blanket.

★ GIANT ENCYCLOPEDIA OF CIRCLE TIME AND GROUP ACTIVITIES

The Class Gallery

5+

*Making every circle the same size and shape establishes a common basis for belonging in the group.
Personal decorations emphasize individuality within the group.*

Words to use

class
group
belonging
unique
special
identical
portrait

Materials

one long sheet of butcher paper
crayons
tape or stapler
display area

What to do

1. Draw a row of identical large circles across the length of the paper, one for each teacher and child in the group.
2. Invite the children to visit the art area and draw a self-portrait in one circle. Demonstrate by drawing a portrait of yourself in a circle.
3. Write each child's name underneath his portrait.
4. The children may decorate the sheet with other drawings as long as the portraits remain clearly visible.
5. Tape the gallery to a wall or staple it to a bulletin board.
6. Conduct a circle time near the gallery. Point out the similarities and differences among portraits. Some may have blond hair, others brown or black. Some or all the faces may be smiling. Invite the children to comment on what they see. Emphasize the uniqueness of each child in the group.

Want to do more?

The children can draw their portraits on separate sheets of construction paper instead of on one long sheet. Also leave space at either end of the sheet for children who may join your group later in the year. Adding their portraits is an excellent way to greet and involve a new child in the group.

Home connection

Send home a section of butcher paper and a description of this activity to help parents and children make a "family gallery."

★ THE PEACEFUL CLASSROOM

Dramatic Play Activities

Eat Your Dinner, Please

3+

Teaches how to set a table and what food children enjoy eating.

Words to use

tablecloth
table
dishes
silverware
food

Materials

tablecloth
dishes and silverware
variety of food pictures cut from magazines
cardboard pieces
glue or tape

What to do

1. Place a tablecloth on the homemaking center table.
2. Provide dishes and silverware for setting the table.
3. Also provide a variety of food pictures which have been cut from magazines and glued to cardboard backing.
4. The scene is set for a re-play of children's experiences with meal time.

★ THE INSTANT CURRICULUM

Bathtime for Baby

3+

Develops an awareness of the needs of babies and how to take care of them.

Words to use

baby   baby tub
washcloth   towel
soap

Materials

towels, washcloths
mild soap
baby tub
washable dolls

What to do

1. Cover a table with towels.
2. Place a baby tub partially filled with water on the table.
3. Provide washable dolls, extra towels, washcloths and mild soap.
4. Let the children bathe babies and redress them.

★ THE INSTANT CURRICULUM

Color House   3+

Explores different colors and the effects of each color.

Words to use

cut
cellophane
color
inside

Materials

large appliance box
scissors
cellophane panels in
    different colors

What to do

1. To create a private space
   for a child, obtain a large
   appliance box.
2. Cut an opening in the
   top of the box. Make
   cellophane panels of different colors to fit this
   opening.
3. Place the box in a lighted area.
4. A child crawls in and discovers the effect of color on the outside world.
5. Change the color panels when appropriate.
6. To create a space ship, use a box big enough for two.

★ THE INSTANT CURRICULUM

Making Wigs

Children love to make wigs to wear in the Housekeeping Center. These creative wigs allow the children to try out new roles and situations while they control the play.

Words to use

panty hose
socks
hair

Materials

panty hose or socks
yarn, strips of paper or cloth
glue

What to do

1. Use panty hose or socks to form the base.
2. Add yarn, strips of paper or cloth to the base to represent different hair styles.
3. Use old tights or socks of different colors to create pig tails, pony tails or fancy top knots.

★ THE COMPLETE LEARNING CENTER BOOK

Designer Clothes

Develops children's creativity by encouraging them to use fabrics to create clothes and costumes.

Words to use

fabric   scarf
attach   clothespin
mirror

Materials

pieces of fabric or scarves
belts or clothespins
basket

What to do

1. Collect pieces of scrap fabric or scarves and place them in a basket.
2. The children tie, push fabric inside belts or attach the cloths with clothespins to create clothes to wear while in the Housekeeping Center.
3. Be sure to include a floor length unbreakable mirror in the Housekeeping Center so the children can admire their creations.

★ THE COMPLETE LEARNING CENTER BOOK

Art Museum   3+

Create a new appreciation for children's artwork with this "museum."

Words to use

boxes   museum
admire   display

Materials

medium-size boxes or large appliance box
tape and glue
paint and brushes
wallpaper, contact paper or fabric

What to do

1. Build a display area for the children's artwork by gluing several medium-size boxes together or by attaching the artwork to an appliance box.
2. Paint these structures with black or bright colors.
3. Cover some boxes with wallpaper, contact paper or fabric.
4. Ask the children to select a picture or creation they would like to display in the Art Museum.

★ THE COMPLETE LEARNING CENTER BOOK

Blossoms

3+

Teaches children about the beauty of flower blossoms.

Words to use

blossom	fruit
trees	silk
arrange	vase

Materials

real blossoms from a pear tree or a flowering fruit tree, or silk blossoms
vases

What to do

1. If you have flowering fruit trees in your play area or within walking distance of the center, go and observe the flowering trees.
2. Cut small branches from flowering trees or use silk blossoms and let the children arrange them for the housekeeping corner and for the snack tables.
3. Discuss how the blossom is the beginning of the fruit.

Want to do more?

The classroom needs to be a place of beauty for the children and their teachers to enjoy. A flower arrangement makes the snack tables special, but it also lets the children know how society values beautiful things from nature. Even the silk reproductions are an attempt to keep alive the beauty of the fragile blossom.

★ STORY S-T-R-E-T-C-H-E-R-S

A Repair Box

3+

Teaches children about tools and how to use them.

Words to use

tool	repair
manual	machine
bill	

Materials

tools	old manuals
receipt book and pen	

What to do

1. Collect tools to "repair" appliances located in the Housekeeping Center.
2. Include a screwdriver, wrench, pliers, wires, screws, bolts and fuses in a plastic bag or fishing tackle box. Caution: Teach children proper use of tools and supervise closely.
3. Place old owner's manuals for appliances in the repair box for children to see diagrams of machine parts and directions for maintenance.
4. A receipt book and pen encourage writing a bill when repairs are completed.

★ THE COMPLETE LEARNING CENTER BOOK

Language Activities

The Three Little Pigs   3+

*Builds vocabulary, demonstrates the number concept of 1-3
and provides texture discovery.*

Words to use

straw
sticks
brick
texture
pig
wolf

Materials

the story "The Three Little Pigs"
straw or hay
sticks
brick

What to do

1. Have a large space prepared for children to role play.
2. Read "The Three Little Pigs." Pass around hay, sticks and a brick at appropriate times during the story. Explore and discuss textures and differences in the materials being passed around.
3. Have children recite together repetitive parts of the story while you read (i.e. "Little pig, little pig, let me come in ..."). Encourage voice changes when wolf speaks and when pig speaks.
4. Let the children role play the story while you re-read the story.
5. Allow children to recite their own version of the story.

Want to do more?

Take turns blindfolding each child with a scarf. Let them touch the straw, sticks and brick. See if they can identify them without seeing them. Younger children may be more comfortable closing their eyes, rather than being blindfolded. Cut out house shapes from poster board. Let children glue hay and sticks to houses. Red aquarium rocks can be used to make the brick house.

★ THE GIANT ENCYCLOPEDIA OF THEME ACTIVITIES

Goldilocks and the Three Bears   3+

Builds children's vocabulary, introduces the number concept 1-3 and the concept of small, medium and large.

Words to use

small
medium
large
bowl
chair
bed

Materials

the story "Goldilocks and the Three Bears"
bowls and spoons (small, medium and large)
towels (small, medium and large)
buttons of various size
lids of various size
containers of various size

What to do

1. Have a large space available for role play.
2. Read "Goldilocks and The Three Bears." Have children recite together repetitive parts of the story. Encourage voice changes when Papa Bear, Mama Bear and Baby Bear speak.
3. Set up bowls and spoons, chairs and towels (for the beds). Allow children to role play the story.
4. Allow children to recite their own version of the story.
5. Put buttons, lids, pots and containers out in groups. Have children arrange each group in order from smallest to largest.

Want to do more?

Cut bear shapes (small, medium and large) out of cardboard or meat trays. Punch holes around edges. Let children lace colored shoe strings or ribbon around the bears. Make oatmeal. Have brown sugar, honey, raisins, cinnamon, etc. available for toppings.

★ THE GIANT ENCYCLOPEDIA OF THEME ACTIVITIES

Magic Mirrors

Builds language and thinking skills as children observe the world through different-colored filters.

Words to use

color
cellophane
mirror

Materials

poster board
florist's cellophane or tinted
   plastic food wrap
scissors
glue or tape

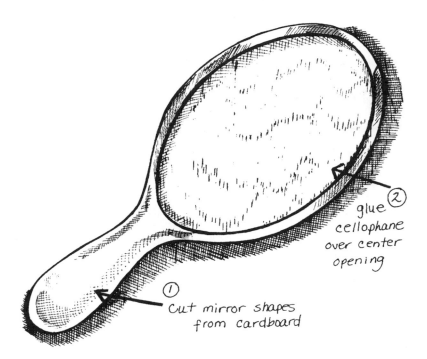

glue ② cellophane over center opening

① Cut mirror shapes from cardboard

What to do

1. Cut mirror shapes from the cardboard. Glue cellophane over center opening, as seen in illustration.
2. During circle time introduce the mirrors.
3. Discuss and act out feelings while looking through the mirrors. Example: blue can make you feel sad. An experience chart can be added for older children. Combine two primary-colored mirrors to make secondary colors. Example: blue and yellow make green.
4. Put the "mirrors" in one of the classroom centers.

★ THE GIANT ENCYCLOPEDIA OF THEME ACTIVITIES

String a Story

Builds vocabulary skills, listening skills and sequence skills.

Words to use

yarn
story
add

Materials

ball of yarn

What to do

1. While holding a ball of yarn in your hands, give the children a story starter. Example: "Yesterday I saw a green monster at the grocery store. He was...."
2. Hold the end of the yarn and pass the ball to a child who will then add a made-up line to the story. When that child is finished, the ball of yarn is passed to another child.

★ THE INSTANT CURRICULUM

Riddle Pictures   3+

Teaches children to select the picture that answers the riddle.

Words to use

animal names
riddle
pictures

Materials

animal pictures
Whose Baby? by Masayuki Yabuuchi
large index cards
rubber cement, tape or glue
tape recorder and tape

What to do

1. Attach pictures of animals to index cards.
2. Tape record some riddles. For example, "I am called a pup. My father is a fox, and my mother is a vixen. Turn the tape off and find my picture." (Fox) "I live in the water and on the shore. My father is called a bull, and my mother is a cow. Find my picture." (Seal) "My father is also called a bull, and my mother is a cow, but I live on land and eat grass. Find my picture." (Bison)
3. Insert some picture riddle cards that the children already know, such as farm animals and pets.
4. Record the instruction, "When you find the picture, turn the tape back on for the next riddle."

Teaching tips

Young preschoolers may need you to present the riddles at first, but after they become accustomed to the activity, they can use the recorder. Although early childhood educators must be collectors, seek assistance from the parents and your friends. Calendars are treasures for science and art lessons. Remember to write in your December and January parent newsletters that you want the families' old calendars for their children's projects.

★ STORY S-t-r-e-t-c-h-e-r-s

Rhyming Words

Encourages children to pair rhyming words heard in Goodnight Moon.

Words to use

rhyme
sounds like

Materials

Goodnight Moon by Margaret Wise Brown

What to do

1. For the children who visit the library corner, reread the section of *Goodnight Moon* where the little bunny is trying to fall asleep and he begins saying rhyming words, "kittens and mittens, toy house and mouse, mush and hush, room and moon, bears and chairs, clocks and socks, house and mouse, brush and mush, air and everywhere."
2. After reading the rhyming section once, read it again pausing to let the children supply the words that rhyme.

Teaching tips

The rhyming exercise in the library corner also can be a follow-up activity in another circle time. Some of the children who enjoy rhyming words may not choose the library corner because they are attracted to other activities. Reading to the children in small groups allows them to enjoy the pictures at a more intimate distance than in a large circle. Observe the children during free play, and if an opportunity arises, ask a few children to come to the library. Afterwards, they can return to the activity of their choice.

★ STORY S-T-R-E-T-C-H-E-R-S

In the Bag

3+

Builds observation skills and vocabulary.

Words to use

describe
guess

Materials

purse, briefcase or bag
assorted items from the classroom or home

What to do

1. Put several items into a purse, briefcase or bag.
2. Children describe the items they find in the purse, briefcase or bag.
3. After the children are experienced, one child can describe the item without letting the other children see it and the other children can try to guess what the item is.

Teaching tips

This activity offers a good opportunity for the teacher to expand the vocabulary of the children by asking questions about each item.

★ THE INSTANT CURRICULUM

Let's Make a Telephone   4+

Encourages children to make telephones and talk to their friends with them.

Words to use

telephone
talk
partner
friend

Materials

round tin cans (Caution: cover sharp edges with duct tape)
nail
hammer
sturdy string
scissors

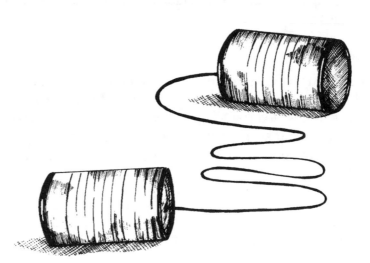

What to do

1. Using the nail, hammer a very small hole in the center of the lid of each can. Give each child a pair of cans and a piece of string about six to eight feet long.
2. The children will then put an end of the string into each hole on the two cans from the outside of the can towards the inside.
3. Help the children knot the ends of the string in each can.
4. Each child picks a partner to talk to.
5. Have each child hold one can and move apart so the string in between the cans is held taut.
6. The pair can talk on the "telephone" they just made. The listener just places her can around her ear and the talker talks into the can.

Want to do more?

The children can play a game of "Guess and Decipher." They guess what their partner just said to them on their new telephone.

★ THE GIANT ENCYCLOPEDIA OF THEME ACTIVITIES

The Magic Pocket

Communication means translating an idea into a form—words or gestures—that can be understood by others. Giving life to ideas through communication is critical to social life, whether we are making friends or resolving conflicts.

Words to use

stories
communication
magic

Materials

What to do

1. Tell the children you are going to pretend to take something out of a magic pocket. You will also pretend to use it. When you are done, you would like to see if they can guess what you took out of the pocket.
2. Take each of the following objects out of your magic pocket and engage in the suggested action. Each time, invite the children to name the imaginary object.
   ✓ hammer a nail
   ✓ throw a ball
   ✓ peel a banana
   ✓ eat a sandwich
   ✓ saw wood
   ✓ cut paper with scissors
   ✓ drink from a glass
3. Ask the children to take turns finding something in their magic pockets to show others in the class. Can other children guess what these objects are?

Want to do more?

Make whatever is in your magic pocket more elaborate. Take out several items with which to set a dinner table or play a game. Try unfolding objects to form much larger items like an automobile or rowboat.

Home connection

Provide parents with instructions for playing "The Magic Pocket" with their children.

★ THE PEACEFUL CLASSROOM

language activities

Body Language

4+

Encourages children to think creatively.

Words to use

communicate
ideas
movements

Materials

chart tablet paper
marker

What to do

1. Brainstorm with the children about ways they use their heads to communicate, for example, shaking yes or no, talking, making facial expressions, listening, etc.
2. List their ideas on chart tablet paper.
3. Talk about ways to communicate that do not use the head, for example, shrugging shoulders, doing hand movements, etc.

★ WHERE IS THUMBKIN?

Math Activities

One Potato, Two Potato, Three Potato, Four

3+

Teaches the counting rhyme. Children can use it to decide turns.

Words to use

potato
fists
partner

Materials

chart tablet or poster board
marker
puzzle or other classroom item

What to do

1. Print the rhyme on a chart tablet or poster board.
2. Teach the children the "One Potato, Two Potato" rhyme used to decide turns.

> *One potato, two potato*
> *Three potato, four,*
> *Five potato, six potato,*
> *Seven potato, more.*

3. Show the children how to make a "potato" with their fists and then, with a partner, to stack them as they say the rhyme. The child with his fist on the top when the rhyme ends with "more" is the winner and gets to select the first puzzle.
4. Discuss with the children that this rhyme is one their parents probably know and used when they were children to decide who goes first.

Want to do more?

Older children can play the elimination hand rhyme with several children.

★ MORE STORY S-T-R-E-T-C-H-E-R-S

e Picking

3+

Teaches children how to discriminate between large and small.

Words to use

large
small

Materials

construction paper
twelve Velcro (1") pieces
scissor
glue
two baskets
poster board, optional

What to do

1. Make a tree (approximately 16" x 20") out of construction paper or draw a tree on poster board, then mount the tree on a bulletin board or on the wall at children's eye level. Glue Velcro pieces to branches.
2. Cut out six large and six small paper apples from construction paper. Glue the other half of Velcro pieces to apples.
3. Place large and small labels on the two baskets (these might be paper apples with words "large" and "small" printed on them).
4. Randomly place large and small apples on tree branches and put the labeled fruit baskets underneath the tree.
5. Explain to the children that apples come in different sizes. Show them the two baskets and the labels on each.
6. Tell the children that they are to "pick" the apples off the tree and put them in the correct baskets according to size.

Want to do more?

Bring out the building blocks and have children separate them into piles according to size.

Book to read

Who Stole the Apples? by S. Heuk

★ THE GIANT ENCYCLOPEDIA OF THEME ACTIVITIES

Counting Seeds

4+

Teaches children that acorns are the seeds of oak trees and uses the acorns to teach one-to-one correspondence.

Words to use

acorns
oak trees
leaves
count
one-to-one correspondence

Materials

The Tiny Seed by Eric Carle
ten acorns
ten leaves
tray

What to do

1. With five children, explain that the acorns that fall in the autumn are the seeds from oak trees.
2. Display a pile of ten acorns piled up on a bed of brightly colored fall leaves. Have the children guess how many acorns are in the pile. Accept any of their guesses, then ask how we can find out how many there are.
3. Count the acorns by moving them from the bed of leaves onto a tray, but pile them again in the center of the tray.
4. Recount by rearranging them into a counting pattern where there is one-to-one correspondence. For example, place one acorn in each hand of every child and then ask how many acorns they have. The children then will count ten hands, not acorns.
5. Rearrange the counting pattern again by placing ten leaves out on the table and having the children place an acorn under each leaf. Ask the children how we can know how many acorns we have without looking at them. We count the leaves instead.

Want to do more?

Encourage children to think of other hidden ways to count, but retain the one-to-one correspondence.

★ Story S-t-r-e-t-c-h-e-r-s

Musical Math   4+

Improves listening skills.

Words to use

listen   counting
directions

Materials

What to do

1. This game is a great counting exercise.
2. Sing the popular song "If You're Happy and You Know It" and change the words to give counting directions.

> *If you're happy and you know it, clap two times...*
> *If you're happy and you know it, hop two times...*
> *If you're happy and you know it, jump four times and snap two times...*

3. Give older children more complicated directions.

★ 500 FIVE MINUTE GAMES

What Made This Shape?   4+

Encourages children to recognize shapes and patterns.

Words to use

pattern   mold

Materials

three or four different containers or different shapes to make three-dimensional sand mold shapes
damp sand

What to do

1. Show the child the different containers.
2. Ask the child to turn her back or close her eyes. Use one of the containers to make a mold.
3. Remove the container and put it back with the others.
4. Ask the child to guess which container you used to make the mold. Then have the child test her guess by making a mold herself using that same container.

Want to do more?

Switch roles. Let the child pick the container and make the mold while you hide your eyes and guess. Encourage the children to play this game with each other. Provide different materials each day.

★ THE OUTSIDE PLAY AND LEARNING BOOK

Seed Sorting

Teaches the math skill of sorting and develops small motor skills.

Words to use

sort
tweezers
seeds

Materials

muffin tin
assorted seeds
tweezers

What to do

1. Provide children with several types of seeds, tweezers and muffin tin.
2. Children pick up the seeds with tweezers and sort them into the muffin tin.

★ THE INSTANT CURRICULUM

This and That

4+

Develops the math skill of classification.

Words to use

like this one   like that one
boy   girl

Materials

masking tape

What to do

1. Place a strip of masking tape on the floor.
2. Have a boy stand on one side of the tape line and a girl on the other.
3. Ask the class what is different about the two people.
4. When someone identifies the distinguishing characteristic as being boy/girl, bring another child up and ask where he or she should go.
5. Give each child a turn.

Want to do more?

Repeat this activity from time to time using other classification criteria, such as type of shoes worn, color of clothing, age, etc. Classification can also be reinforced with everyday activities (all the children with white shoes may go to the snack table).

★ THE INSTANT CURRICULUM

SEPTEMBER

math activities

57

Inch by Inch

4+

Encourages the development of measurement skills.

Words to use

inch
exact
match
compare

Materials

tape or paint
marker
assorted items such as a
straw, a comb, cardboard
tube, cube, etc.

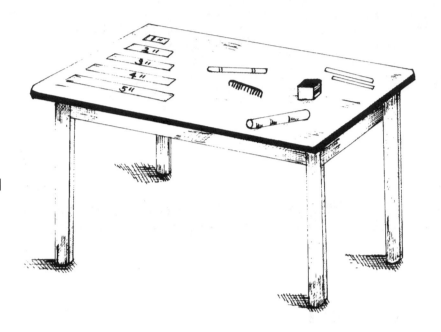

What to do

1. Tape or paint lines on a classroom table one inch apart.
2. Number the lines one-inch, two-inch, etc.
3. Provide a variety of objects that are exact in inch measurements. (5" straw, 4" comb, 3" tube, 1" cube, etc.)
4. Children match objects to lines and compare lengths.

Want to do more?

Holiday adaptation: Cut strips of construction paper in 1", 2", 3", 4", and 5" lengths. Children paste the strips on art paper to simulate Christmas candles of varying length. Flames can be added with paint, crayon or construction paper.

★ THE INSTANT CURRICULUM

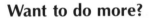

Coins

Here's a simple song to help children recognize different coins and their value.

Words to use

penny
nickel
dime
quarter
bank

Materials

pennies, nickels, dimes and quarters—enough to give each child one coin
a piggy bank or other type of coin bank

What to do

1. Show each coin to the children and tell them its worth. Review several times.
2. Sing "The Coin Song" and hold up the appropriate coin as you sing about it.

> *"The Coin Song" (to the tune of "Shortening Bread")*
> *A penny is one cent, one cent, one cent*
> *A penny is one cent, I know that!*
> *A nickel is five cents ...*
> *A dime is ten cents ...*
> *A quarter is twenty-five cents ...*

3. Give one coin to each child. Sing "The Coin Song" again. After each verse, have the children with the appropriate coins bring them up and deposit them in the bank, one by one. Continue to sing the appropriate verse as they do this. Sing the other verses and have the children with those coins put them in the bank. Continue until all coins are collected.
4. Redistribute the coins and continue playing for as long as the children are interested.

Want to do more?

With a small group, give each child a handful of different coins. Sing any one of the verses of "The Coin Song," but instead of "I know that!" substitute "(child's name) has (number)." Allow the child to fill in the blank by telling you the number of coins that were just mentioned that he or she has.

★ THE GIANT ENCYCLOPEDIA OF THEME ACTIVITIES

Piggy Bank

4+

Children will love making these useful piggy banks. This activity complements a study of money, but also makes a nice gift.

Words to use

piggy bank
money
save

Materials

paperboard salt container
  or other canister with
  pour spout, one per child
single egg cups (cut from
  an egg carton)
black buttons or large round
  black stickers
pink paint and paintbrushes
6" black pipe cleaners
pink construction paper cut
  in 2" squares
scissors
glue

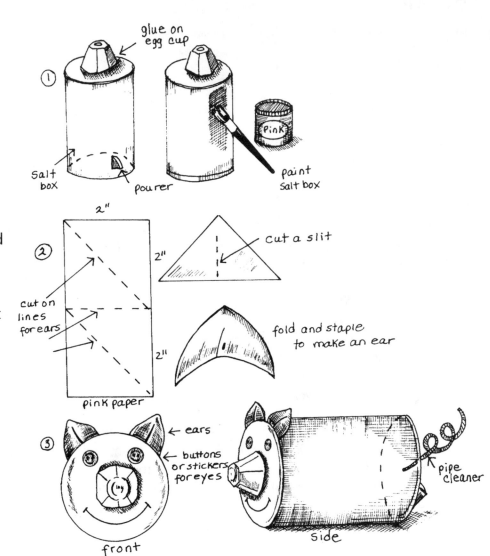

What to do

1. Glue the egg cup to the bottom of the salt box on the end opposite the pour spout. This will be the pig's nose.
2. Paint the whole pig pink and let dry completely.
3. While painted box is drying, cut the pink construction paper square diagonally to make ears.
4. For eyes, glue buttons or apply stickers on each side of the face above the nose.
5. Glue the two ears on top of the head.
6. To make the tail, first poke a small hole in the other end of the canister with scissors or a nail. Then curl the pipe cleaner around a finger or a pencil and insert it.
7. The spout is for putting money in the piggy bank.

★ THE GIANT ENCYCLOPEDIA OF THEME ACTIVITIES

Music and Movement Activities

The Pear Tree

3+

Teaches children to perform the motions of the poem.

Words to use

move
stretch
pinch
fingers

Materials

What to do

1. Teach the children the poem with motions: arms in a circle showing how big the hole was for the seed, fingers pinched together showing the tiny seed, arms in a circle with hands stretched overhead and fingertips touching to show the sun, arms outstretched for the branches, and thumb and index finger making a circle to show the size of the blossom.
2. Recite:

> This is the hole I dug so round.
> This is the seed I put in the ground.
> This is the sun shining so.
> This is the pear tree starting to grow.
> These are the limbs stretching up high
> These are the blossoms, so pretty, oh my.
> I think I see a green one there
> Just wait, it will ripen into a pear.
> By Shirley Raines

3. Practice the poem and movements several times.

Want to do more?

Build your repertoire of fingerplays, songs, poems and chants not only to help children recall information, but also to fill those moments when children have to wait before a new activity can begin.

★ STORY S-T-R-E-T-C-H-E-R-S

Here We Go 'Round the Apple Tree

3+

Teaches children to sing different words to a familiar song.

Words to use

apple tree
'round
substitute

Materials

What to do

1. Sing "Here We Go 'Round the Mulberry Bush." Then teach the children the words you want to substitute.
2. Sing—

> *Here we go 'round the apple tree, the apple tree, the apple tree*
> *Here we go 'round the apple tree, so early in the morning.*
>
> *Here we go arranging flowers, arranging flowers, arranging flowers,*
> *Here we go arranging flowers, so early in the spring.*
>
> *Here we go building a tree house, building a tree house, building a tree house,*
> *Here we go building a tree house, just in time for summer.*
>
> *Here we go picking apples, picking apples, picking apples,*
> *Here we go picking apples, so late in the fall.*
>
> *Here we go baking pies, baking pies, baking pies,*
> *Here we go baking pies, all winter, all winter long.*
> *Adapted by Shirley Raines*

Want to do more?

Let the children suggest hand motions and body movements to accompany the song.

★ STORY S-T-R-E-T-C-H-E-R-S

Shakers

Teaches rhythm, coordination and listening skills.

Words to use

dried beans
plastic egg
shake

Materials

dried beans
plastic egg
masking tape

What to do

1. Make shakers by putting dried beans inside plastic eggs and taping them closed. These make perfect shakers.
2. Sing "If You're Happy and You Know It" with the children. They can use the shakers for the places in the song where there are claps and stomps.

★ WHERE IS THUMBKIN?

Leaf Dance

Exercises large muscles allowing children to move freely in creative dance. Additionally, the children will see the creation of the color orange by combining red and yellow.

Words to use

leaf
red and yellow
toss
twirl

Materials

heavy black marker
scissors
large sheet of plain newsprint or
    classified ad section of
    newspaper
red tempera paint
yellow tempera paint
medium-sized brushes
"The Gentle Sea" by Hap Palmer
record or tape player

What to do

1. Using the marker, draw the outline of a large simple leaf on the paper. Make one for each child. Cut out the leaf or ask children with good cutting skills to cut out the leaves.
2. Each child uses red and yellow paint to paint one side of the giant leaf. Allow to dry overnight.
3. Gather children together in a large open area such as a gym. Tell the children that they are going to use the leaves they painted to participate in a leaf dance.
4. Play the record or tape of "The Gentle Sea" by Hap Palmer and have the children listen to the music. Explain that when the music goes up, they may want to toss their leaves into the air. When the music goes down, they may want to fall to the ground with their leaves. When the music seems to twirl, they can twirl around.
5. Give each child a leaf. Once again start a record or tape and let the dance begin!

Want to do more?

Choose a classical recording such as a waltz or "Autumn Leaves" by Roger Williams to do another dance.

★ THE GIANT ENCYCLOPEDIA OF THEME ACTIVITIES

Musical Beanbags   3+

Children must listen very carefully during this activity.

Words to use

beanbag
music
head
shoulder
elbow
freeze

Materials

beanbag
record and record player or taped music

What to do

1. Give each child a beanbag.
2. Put on a record. Children move around the room with the beanbag on their head, on their shoulder or on their elbow, while music is playing.
3. When the music stops, the children "freeze" holding the position they are in until the teacher resumes playing the record.

★ THE INSTANT CURRICULUM

Science Activities

Spyglass Treasure Hunt: Close-up and Far Away   3+

Encourages children to take long distance and close-up looks at their world and discover the new things that can be seen through these special windows. This limiting perspective reveals beauty that is often hidden by the overwhelming visual stimuli in an environment. Focusing on one flower in a field of many helps children become aware of the little things that together make a whole.

Words to use

focus
telescope
view
cylinder

Materials

paper rolls such as from toilet paper, paper towels, foil or wrapping paper
magnifiers such as telescope, binoculars, microscope, optional
paper and pen or tape recorder

What to do

1. Choose an observation site. A familiar place might be particularly enjoyable.
2. Once destination is reached, provide each child with a viewer (paper rolls in a variety of lengths and sizes).
   Caution: Walking while looking through viewers can be dangerous.
3. Sit down and choose something to observe, such as a large tree. Sit close enough so that only a small portion of the tree can be seen through the tube.
4. Have a child focus on a spot and describe what is seen. Can others find it?
5. An adult should record observations on paper or tape for later comparison, discussion and reconstruction of the object. Move closer or farther away and repeat the activity. What changes?

Want to do more?

Find a spot and explore it close up with a tube. Get closer with a magnifier. Get even closer with a microscope. Try long distance followed by binocular and telescope viewing. Take close-up and long distance photographs of the same object and match the part to the whole. Experiment with a variety of angles for viewing—everything from a bug's eye to a bird's eye view.

★ HUG A TREE

Spinner Helicopter

3+

This aircraft is really a glider whose two airfoils catch enough air to slow their descent. Given a source of power, they could climb up and fly away. Based on seeds whose natural structures produce similar effects, the spinner can gracefully circle to the ground, giving children another glimpse at an attempt to mimic a natural event. Find an ash or maple seed and see the similarity.

Words to use

fly
spin
helicopter

Materials

paper
paper clip
scissors
drawing of model
(see illustration)

What to do

1. Make the spinner as illustrated.
2. Hold it up as high as you can.
3. Drop it and watch it fall. What happens?

Want to do more?

Collect seeds from maple trees. Watch them as they fall. What's the biggest or smallest working spinner you can make? What happens when you add more paper clips? Can you make one from something besides paper?

★ MORE MUDPIES TO MAGNETS

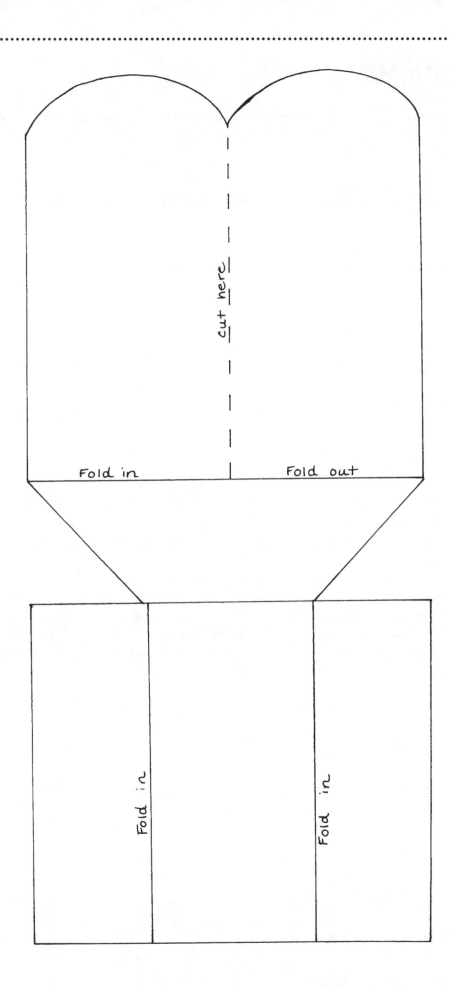

Playing with Mud

3+

There is nothing like mud! You can pat it, shape it, dribble it, pour it and change it. After special communication with parents, let children experience the joy of this messy but wonderful material.

Words to use

mud
squish
mess

Materials

small wading pool
low table
several dish tubs
sand, dirt
water source
pitchers
various spoons, measuring cups, sand play toys

What to do

1. Place the wading pool on top of a low table so that the children stand around the edge to play, rather than climbing inside it. Put the dish tubs inside the wading pool. Drips and spills, therefore, fall into the wading pool, minimizing the mess. (This activity could be set up without the wading pool—simply put the dish tubs side by side around the table.)
2. If possible, locate several different textures of sand and dirt. Fill the dish tubs with these. You might leave one empty.
3. Let the children fill the pitchers with water from an outside faucet or trickling hose, and then mix it with the sand in the dish tubs. Give them just the basic instructions to get them started, and they can make their own discoveries. Let them mix the different kinds of sand and dirt as they wish.
4. Give the children access to a wide range of sand play toys so they can pick out what they need.
5. Present this in the morning. See what happens if you leave it out in the sun during lunch time and rest time, and then return to it in the afternoon.

Want to do more?

Vary the sand toys. Put measuring cups, spoons and bowls out one day. Another day provide rocks and play dishes or plastic animals and people.

★ THE OUTSIDE PLAY AND LEARNING BOOK

Texture Box

3

Teaches children to use their sense of touch to identify materials they cannot see.

Words to use

feel
texture
smooth
scratchy
rough
soft

Materials

a variety of materials with different textures
shoe box
glue
blindfold

What to do

1. Collect a variety of materials that have different textures. Materials with an interesting texture include burlap, foil, sandpaper, silk, corduroy, yarn, cork pieces, bark, cotton balls and screen.
2. Select and glue the textured materials onto cardboard shoe boxes.
3. The children blindfold each other, then try to identify the textures they are touching.

★ THE COMPLETE LEARNING CENTER BOOK

Sequencing the Seasons

4

Teaches children to arrange pictures of the seasons in their sequence.

Words to use

fall
winter
spring
summer
sequence

Materials

pictures depicting the various seasons
scissors
large index cards
rubber cement, tape or glue
hole puncher
long shoe laces or yarn

What to do

1. From magazines, catalogs and calendars, have the children cut out pictures depicting the seasons. Attach their pictures to index cards.
2. Ask the children to arrange their cards in the order of the seasons. Do not tell them where to begin. If they begin in fall, have them place the winter card next, and so on.
3. After they have practiced arranging the season sequence cards, punch two holes at the top of the card, one hole in each corner. Then punch two at the bottom of the card.
4. Demonstrate how to lace the cards together. Tie a big knot in one end of a shoe lace or yarn and lace it through the top right hand hole of the fall card at the top, put the lace on the back side of the card, and then lace it through the bottom right hand hole at the bottom of the card. Next, lace the top of the winter card, then at the bottom, and so on. Tie a knot in the lace at the end. Repeat with another piece of yarn with the holes on the left hand side. Hold it up and see the season pictures in order.

Want to do more?

Laminate the cards to make them durable for a lot of practice. Also try lacing other cards for sequencing tasks.

★ STORY S-T-R-E-T-C-H-E-R-S

Composting   4+

Develops the ability to form conclusions from guessing and observation.

Words to use

observe
guess
dig
compare

Materials

plastic packaging
lettuce leaves
one shovel
one apple core
Styrofoam pieces
paper and pencil
The Compost Heap by Harlow Rockwell

What to do

1. If necessary, get permission to dig four holes in the ground. Make sure the secured place is a safe and isolated one.
2. Read the book aloud to the class.
3. Ask the children how long they think it would take for a lettuce leaf, an apple core, a piece of Styrofoam and a piece of plastic packaging to decompose. Write down their responses.

4. To add excitement to this activity, go outside and dig four holes in the ground. Drop a lettuce leaf in one hole, a piece of plastic packaging in another, an apple core in the third and a piece of Styrofoam in the fourth. Fill the holes with dirt and mark the holes.
5. In one month dig up the four items and compare and contrast the children's guesses with the actual results.
6. Make a compost pile from scraps used in your classroom (apple peelings, banana peels). In the springtime, use the compost to grow flowers or vegetables.

★ THE GIANT ENCYCLOPEDIA OF THEME ACTIVITIES

Planting Bulbs   4+

Teaches how bulbs develop.

Words to use

bulb   food
water   sunlight

Materials

bulbs: tulips, crocus, gladiolus, daffodil, onion
shovel
mulch
ruler

What to do

1. Talk about things that grow—people, animals, plants, insects.
2. Show and discuss the bulbs: tulip, crocus, daffodil, gladiolus and onion. Talk about the different sizes. Show pictures of the flowers.
3. With each different bulb show where the roots, stem and skin is. Cut one bulb in half to show the beginning of the plant inside.
4. How deep do we have to plant them? Show 6 inches (tulip and crocus) and 10 inches (gladiolus).
5. Prepare the soil with mulch. Dig the holes. Plant bulbs right way: roots down, stem up. Put in bone meal. Cover. Water regularly.
6. Wait a long time until spring! It's worth it!

Want to do more?

Talk about seedlings, saplings and trees. Or the parts of a plant: roots, stem, flower and leaves. Or the parts of a flower: petals, pistil, stamen, pollen, calyx and corolla. Or the parts of a leaf: stem, vein and tip.

Books to read

Planting a Rainbow by Lois Ehlert
The Reason for a Flower by Ruth Heller
The Tiny Seed by Eric Carle
Trees by Harry Behm and James Endicott

science activities

71

Songs to sing

"Because It's Spring"
"In the Leafy Tree Tops"
"Popcorn Popping"
"Springtime Is Coming"

★ THE GIANT ENCYCLOPEDIA OF THEME ACTIVITIES

Paper Airplanes

4+

Teaches children how to make paper airplanes.

Words to use

fold
paper
fly
compare

Materials

heavy typing paper
scissors
yarn or twine

What to do

1. At free play time, with small groups of children, make paper airplanes. Fold the airplanes one fold at a time, with the children duplicating your folds.
2. When finished, conduct test flights in an open area of the classroom.
3. Measure one of the longest flights by cutting a piece of yarn or twine the length of the flight.
4. Take the paper airplanes outside and test fly them again.
5. Measure the distance of the outside flight by cutting a piece of yarn or twine the length of the flight.
6. Compare the differences in lengths for the inside and outside flights.

Teaching tips

To avoid competition, simply place all the airplanes on the table in a row and have the children select one, rather than the one he or she made.

★ STORY S-T-R-E-T-C-H-E-R-S

Inverted Glass Experiment   4+

Teaches how to follow the directions of the experiment and observe what happens.

① add food coloring to bowl of water.

② stuff paper napkin in glass.

③ turn glass upside down and push all the way under the water.

④ have children observe that napkin is dry.

Words to use

experiment   observe
upside down   dry
wet

Materials

Air Is All Around You by Franklyn M. Branley
large, clear mixing bowl
food coloring
paper napkins
glass

What to do

1. Follow the directions in the book, which are:
   ✓ put water in a big bowl
   ✓ color the water with a little bit of food coloring
   ✓ stuff a paper napkin into the bottom of a glass
   ✓ turn the glass upside down
   ✓ keep the glass upside down, make sure it is straight up and down, do not tip it
   ✓ push it all the way under the water
   ✓ lift the glass out of the water, and
   ✓ turn it right side up and take out the napkin
2. Have the children observe that the napkin is dry.
3. Let all the children who want to do the experiment have a turn.

Teaching tips

Remember that young children are hands-on learners. They will learn more if they do the experiment themselves. Many of the children will not understand what the experiment demonstrates, but they enjoy following directions and getting the same results as the teacher. Also, avoid referring to this experiment as magic or as a trick. While it may seem phenomenal, it is natural.

★ STORY S-T-R-E-T-C-H-E-R-S

Curves and Straights   5+

Children discover that circles, triangles and squares are forms created by the natural world. Searching for these shapes in nature reinforces the identification of the basic forms and promotes visual perception skills.

Words to use

circle
rectangle
square
triangle
shape

Materials

circle, triangle, rectangle and square shapes drawn on cardboard
glue or paste
poster board

What to do

1. Give out shape cards.
2. This is a hunt. Find a shape in nature that closely resembles the shape on the card. Collect the objects (nuts—round, redbud leaves—heart shape, bark—often rectangular).
3. When all the shapes have been found, go to a spot where you have laid out glue and poster board. Divide the poster board into sections; one section for each shape.
4. Each child pastes his or her shape on the appropriate board for a shapes collage. You can add to this as new items are found.

Want to do more?

Find objects that have more than one shape. Have a shape bingo game. As the shapes are found add them to the bingo card. Find objects to match solid figures such as cylinders, boxes, cubes, balls. Place an object in front of a light to determine the shape of its shadow. Try to predict the shape it will cast. Move the object around. The shadow may change shape.

★ HUG A TREE

Snack and Cooking Activities

Rice Cake Creatures   3+

This fun activity allows children to make special snacks that are good for them.

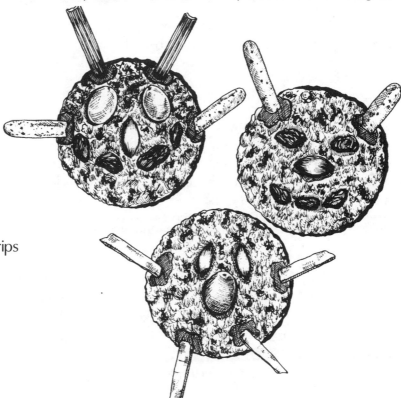

Words to use

nutritious
creature
imagination

Materials

miniature rice cakes
peanut butter
raisins or currants
pretzel sticks
sliced almonds
thinly sliced carrot or celery strips
green grapes
cream cheese
plates
bowls or plates for ingredients
butter knives
lots of napkins

What to do

1. Place two rice cakes on each plate and give each child a small knife (plastic works fine). Julienne the vegetables to use as whiskers and cut the grapes in half to be rabbit tails. Put almonds, vegetables, currants and pretzels into several bowls to be shared.
2. Demonstrate a rice mouse to children: spread peanut butter on a rice cake, use currents for eyes and a nose, half-almonds for ears, vegetables for whiskers and a pretzel for a tail.
3. Demonstrate a bunny to children: spread cream cheese on the rice cake, use almonds for ears, currents for eyes, vegetables for whiskers and grape halves for tails.
4. Let the children prepare their own animals, making whatever creations they choose.

Want to do more?

Any variety of healthy, little ingredients can be used to create any variety of creatures. Apple rounds or small crackers or shapes of bread can be used as the base. Cheese spread and other nut butters can be used as the "fur." Frosting can be used too, but only for special events.

★ THE GIANT ENCYCLOPEDIA OF THEME ACTIVITIES

Country Apples

3+

Children will learn the names and tastes of different kinds of apples.

Words to use

golden   red
delicious   green
sweet   tangy
tart

Materials

golden delicious apples   red delicious apples
green cooking apples   knives and cutting boards
baskets

What to do

1. If possible, let the children help you shop for the apples. If not, bring the apples to the classroom in a grocery bag. Let the children help you wash the apples.
2. Other children can arrange a variety of apples in a basket for each snack table.
3. During snack, cut slices from the kind of apple the child picks out. Then ask him to try at least one other kind and tell you how it tastes.
4. Remember to use descriptive words such as sweet, tangy, tart.

Want to do more?

You can extend the apple tasting snack by polling the children and deciding which apple is the class favorite. Do a simple mathematical graph by having each child select a strip of construction paper that is the same color as the type of apple he likes. Each child then glues the strips onto a poster and the class can compare visually or count and decide what their favorite kind of apple is. This graph is both a prenumber and a numerical graph.
(Adapted from an activity in Penny Clem's classroom.)

★ STORY S-T-R-E-T-C-H-E-R-S

Fancy Cutting

3+

This is a fun thing for the teacher to do at snack time or if someone brings an apple for lunch.
Children will watch in amazement and be delighted by the results.

Words to use

cut
crowns
puzzles
stars
mushrooms

cut →

Materials

apples
sharp knife

What to do

1. **Crowns**: Make sure the apple is washed. Using a sharp knife, cut apple crowns by cutting pattern one all the way around the middle. Be sure to cut well into the center of the apple but not all the way through. Hold the top and bottom of the apple. Give a twist and pull the halves apart! Surprise! Two crowns. The children will have fun putting them together and taking them apart again.
2. **Puzzles**: Cut puzzles by cutting a pattern all the way around the apple. Continue as with crowns.
3. **Stars**: Children (and many adults!) are amazed to find that there is a star inside of every apple. Just cut the apple horizontally, and you will find it . Enjoy this wonder by cutting the snack apples right at the table with the children, rather than cutting them ahead of time. Another way to find the three-dimensional star inside each apple (and pear) is to eat the apple whole. When you begin to get close to the core, nibble gingerly so that you get as much pulp as possible off the little core, or seed house, without actually disturbing it. Let this seed house dry and you have a three-dimensional five-pointed star. This, again, provides pure wonder for the children if you bring it to them in a "wonder full" way. It's also a great way to encourage them to eat their whole apple!
4. **Mushrooms**: Make a horizontal cut all the way around the apple, just below the center. Then make four straight cuts from the bottom of the apple down to the horizontal cut, as if you were cutting a square around the core. Take off these straight cut pieces, turn the apple right side up and you have a mushroom.

★ EARTHWAYS

Something Special for You

3+

Here's the perfect story to tell before snack—especially if apples are on the menu. There's a surprise at the end of this "tell and draw" story that all the children will enjoy.

Words to use

draw
apple
surprise

Materials

large sheet of paper and marker or chalkboard and chalk
grocery sack
apples
knife

What to do

1. Place the apples in the grocery sack, along with the knife.
2. Draw the following illustrations on the paper or chalkboard as you tell the story.

> *"Something Special for You"*
>
> *Once there was a little old lady who lived in the mountains in a little house right here. One day she decided to go down the mountain to town, so she left her house and started down the road like this.*
>
> *On the way she met (child's name), and he asked, "Where are you going on such a fine day?" "I'm going down to town," replied the little old lady. "What are you going to get?" asked (child's name). "You'll just have to wait and see," said the lady.*
>
> *On she walked until she met (child's name) and (child's name), and the other boys and girls. They all asked her, "Where are you going on such a fine day?" "I'm going down to town," she replied. "What are you going to get?" they asked. "You'll just have to wait and see," the lady told them. The little old lady finally got to town. She went in the store and she came out with a big bag. (At this point, take out the bag and hold it up.)*
>
> *She started back up the mountain like this, when all the boys and girls came running up to her. "What did you get? What's in your bag?" they all begged. "I've got some stars," the little old lady answered. "Come home with me and I'll give you each one."*

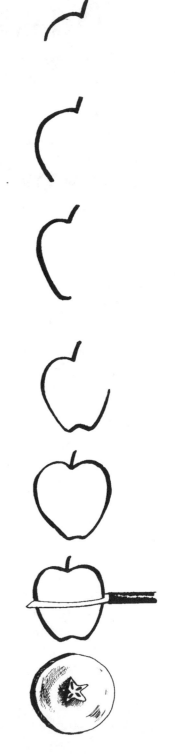

So the little old lady and all the boys and girls continued up the mountain like this. They finally reached her house, and she opened her bag and pulled out an apple. (Open the bag and take out an apple and the knife.)

"But where are the stars?" questioned the children. The little old lady took the knife, cut the apple in half, and showed the children a beautiful star inside the apple. (Cut the apple in half horizontally and show the children the star.) Then she cut all the apples in half and gave all the children a star of their very own!

Want to do more?

Talk about how the children are like apples. They are all different on the outside, but there's a special star in each of them. Encourage them to share what's special about them on the inside.

★ TRANSITION TIME

Baking Whole Apples   3+

Baking apples whole or turning them into cake are two delicious ways to bring autumn's harvest into the classroom.

Words to use

apple	bake
cinnamon	grated nutmeg
core	

Materials

large apples (preferably organic so the skins can be eaten)
goodies for stuffing: chopped walnuts, raisins, date pieces, currants, etc.
cinnamon or nutmeg
sweeteners: honey, brown sugar, maple syrup or sucanat
large bowl and mixing spoon
apple corers
large baking pan
milk or cream, optional

What to do

1. Wash and dry the apples.
2. Mix the stuffing ingredients with a bit of cinnamon and/or fresh grated nutmeg and small amount of sweetener.
3. Have the children use the corers to core the apples.
4. After putting the cores in the compost bucket, stuff each apple with the stuffing mixture. Children love to do this, and even the youngest can help.
5. Place the apples in a baking dish and add about 1/4 inch of water.
6. Bake the apples in an oven at 350°F for about an hour.
7. Serve in bowls with a bit of milk or cream if you like. A hearty and delicious snack!

★ EARTHWAYS

snack & cooking activities

Baby Apple Pies

3+

Encourages children to learn how to prepare apple pies for snack.

Words to use

apple pie
muffin tin
pie crust

Materials

premixed pie crusts	knife
flour	saucepan
wooden spoon	rolling pin
muffin tins	shortening
apple pie filling	

What to do

1. Turn the muffin tins upside down. Grease and lightly flour the bottoms of the cups of the muffin tins.
2. Cut circles from the pie crusts just the size to fit over the bottoms of the muffin tin cups.
3. Let the children take the pie crust circles and shape them over the bottom of the muffin tin cups.
4. Bake the baby pie crusts following the directions on the pie crust package, shortening the baking time slightly.
5. Remove the baby pie crusts from the oven, and take them off the bottoms of the tins to cool.
6. Heat the apple pie filling in a saucepan. Fill the baby pie crusts. An optional step is to add a topping.

Want to do more?

On another day, invite a parent who enjoys baking to come to class and prepare an apple pie from scratch. The parent can work at a table and children can come and go during free play, but be certain each child participates in some step of the preparation. (Adapted from Lisa Lewis's classroom.)

★ STORY S-t-r-e-t-c-h-e-r-s

Pear Treats

3+

Encourages children to prepare a variety of snacks with pears.

Words to use

pears
snack
cut
slices

Materials

fresh ripe pears	baskets
canned pear halves	large serving bowl
raisins	small bowls and spoons
coconut	mixed nuts

What to do

1. Invite several children to assist with the preparation of the special snack time. Ask them to wash the ripe pears and arrange them in baskets for the snack table.
2. Cut some of the fresh ripe pear halves for the children to see the seeds. Then cut slices from the fresh pears for everyone to taste.
3. Open the canned pears and let the other children pour them into large serving bowls. The children then serve themselves from the large bowl.
4. Have everyone compare the tastes of the fresh pears with the canned ones.
5. Let the children sprinkle a variety of toppings onto their canned pear halves (for example, coconut, raisins, mixed nuts), then compare the tastes.

Want to do more?

Vary the toppings on other days and have brown sugar or nutmeg, grated cheese or cottage cheese, but let the children choose whether to have their pears plain or with toppings.

★ STORY S-T-R-E-T-C-H-E-R-S

Baking Bread 3+

Teaches children how bread is made and prepares a delicious snack.

Words to use

yeast	rise
knead	loaves

Materials

1-2 tablespoons active dry yeast
1/3 cup plus 1 teaspoon honey
warm water
small mixing bowl
1 teaspoon salt
1/3 cup oil, plus a little extra for greasing the bowl and pan(s)
6 cups whole wheat flour, supplemented as needed
two large bowls and wooden spoons
measuring spoons and cups
wooden board or clean table top
clean cloth
two loaf pans or baking trays

What to do

1. In a small bowl, mix the yeast, 1 teaspoon honey and 1/2 cup warm water. Allow this mixture to sit until it gets bubbly—approximately ten minutes.
2. In a large bowl, mix 1 1/2 cups warm water, 1/3 cup oil, 1/3 cup honey and salt.
3. Pour the yeast mixture into the large bowl and stir in three cups of whole wheat flour. Mix well, and continue adding more flour until the dough is fairly stiff and not sticky (depending on the humidity, type of flour, etc., you may need to add up to three more cups of flour).
4. Turn the dough onto a lightly floured board or clean table top and begin to knead, firmly pressing the dough away from you with the heels of your hands, folding it back onto itself and pressing it away from you again. Continue rhythmically kneading the dough until it becomes smooth and elastic. Give the children small balls of dough to knead. Just break off some dough for each child who wants to help, and roll all the pieces back into one big ball when the kneading is finished. The children often like to have a turn kneading the big ball of dough!
5. Place dough in an oiled bowl, cover with a clean cloth and let rise on a sunny window sill or in another warm place until it doubles in bulk (about 45 minutes).
6. Punch down (press down two or three times firmly but gently with your fist). Shape into two loaves or 24 small rolls (approximately). Cover and let rise once more for about 20-30 minutes.
7. Bake at 350°F for 45-50 minutes for bread or 20 minutes for rolls. Note: You can leave out one or both risings (steps five and six) if you want to eat the bread or rolls for snack the same day. Just have the children roll handfuls of dough into balls and place them on an oiled cookie sheet. Bake them right away, and you'll have warm, fresh rolls in 20 minutes. Make sure to let them cool a bit before eating. The children love to break the rolls open and watch the steam come out.

★ EARTHWAYS

Three Bears Porridge   3+

Teaches children how to follow directions.

Words to use

recipe
directions
cook
oatmeal

Materials

oatmeal	electric pot
water	salt
measuring cups	spoons
bowls	honey or brown sugar
timer	paper
marker	laminating film or clear contact paper

What to do

1. Draw the recipe using pictures (see page 259 for making rebus recipes), following the directions on the oatmeal box. Laminate or cover with contact paper if possible.
2. Follow the directions and allow each child a chance to stir.
   Caution: The cooking pot will need close supervision.
3. Serve for snack with honey or brown sugar.

Want to do more?

For variation add raisins, diced apples or nuts.

★ THEMESTORMING

Drying Apples   4+

Drying apples is a way to harvest nature's bounty in the fall and save it up for winter. If you have access to an apple tree or trees, all the better. (Ask parents, check in the yellow pages or with the local extension office for field trip possibilities.) Then the children can do the picking as well.

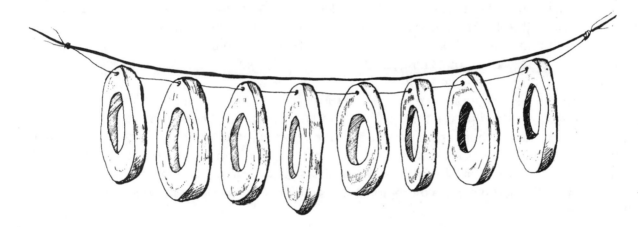

Words to use

dried
shrink
string

Materials

10-12 whole apples, organically grown if possible
sink or small dishpan
towels
basket or bowl
vegetable peelers
sharp knife for the teacher
small knives for children—regular table knives will work but look for smaller size real knives, sometimes called luncheon knives, or buy paring knives and "predull" them
small cutting boards
small bowl
large needles and thread
dowels, optional

What to do

1. Fill the sink or a small dishpan with water and put the apples in it.
2. Let the children rinse them, dry them and place them in a basket.
3. Bring the apples to the table and peel them with the children, using the vegetable peelers (the apples dry more effectively with the skins removed).
4. With the sharp knife, the teacher slices the peeled apples horizontally into 1/4 inch thick slices. Surprise! Notice the star in the center of the apple. Have the children cut around the center to remove the star and seeds. You will end up with apple slices with a round hole in the center.
5. Using pieces of thread about as long as your arm, thread large needles with doubled thread, knot-ting the thread about three inches from the end,
6. "Sew" through the first apple slice by going through the center hole and then back through the doubled thread. This will secure the apple by knotting it to the end of the thread.
7. After securing the first apple slice, have the children continue the "sewing." They sew right through the apple pulp, slide the slice down toward the last apple slice and then sew back up through the doubled thread. Leave a bit of space between each slice so that air can circulate between them.
8. Each thread is finished when no more apple slices will fit. Knot the last slice in place as you did the first.
9. Hang the strings of apples in the room to dry. Possible places are from plant hangers; from the har-vest wreath if you have one; from hooks attached to the ceiling; from a closet pole or a broom-stick attached to the ceiling at each end so that it hangs horizontally. This will accommodate lots of strings of drying apples.
Note: It is important that the apple slices do not hang in strong, direct sunlight, so that the slices can air dry slowly. Also, each slice should be separated from the next so that air can circulate around it. If you have lots of slices that are close together, they can get moldy before they are able to dry out. If the slices are slipping together on the string, you may need to adjust them or knot them in place.
Alternative Method: If you'd like to avoid the stringing process, you can hang the apples horizontally by threading them onto a thin dowel. Hang the dowel by supporting each end. You can fit lots of apple slices on a single dowel, and even the youngest children can help.

★ EARTHWAYS

Transition Activities

Please and Thank You

3+

Helps children learn common courtesies they can use at meals and throughout the day. Good manners enable children to be accepted in different social situations.

Words to use

please
thank you
excuse me
manners
polite

Materials

What to do

1. Talk about manners and why it is important to be polite.
2. Help the children understand the connection between their behavior and how others perceive them by role-playing and using puppets to act out classroom situations.
3. Discuss when to say "please," "thank you" and "excuse me," then sing the following song to the tune of "My Bonnie Lies Over the Ocean."

> *There are two magic words*
> *That open any door with ease.*
> *One little word is "thanks."*
> *The other word is "please."*
>
> *Thank you, thank you,*
> *Thank you and please.*
> *Thank you, thank you,*
> *Thank you and please.*

Want to do more?

Practice answering the telephone, meeting new people and other social situations which call for good manners.

★ TRANSITION TIME

Nutkin

3+

Nutkin helps quiet children for a story or other activity. Children's auditory discrimination skills are strengthened as they listen for Nutkin.

Words to use

nuts
squirrel
gray

Materials

potato chip canister or similar can
    with a lid
brown and gray construction paper
assorted nuts
popsicle stick
scissors
markers
tape

What to do

1. Cover the can with brown paper to resemble a tree trunk.
2. Put a handful of nuts in the bottom of the can.
3. Draw and cut a squirrel from the gray construction paper and tape it to the end of the popsicle stick.
4. Place the squirrel puppet in the can with the nuts and put on the lid.
5. As the children sit down for circle or story, take the can and say, "I wonder if Nutkin is at home. If you're quiet maybe you can hear him rattling his nuts."
6. Shake the can.
7. When all the children are focused, quietly pull the little squirrel puppet out and let it introduce a new activity or tell the children a story.

Want to do more?

Hide nuts on the playground, and let the children try and find them like squirrels. Count and sort the nuts in the can, or use them for other math activities.

★ TRANSITION TIME

Kings, Queens and Helpers

This idea gives different children turns to be a leader or a classroom helper each day. In addition to building responsibility and contributing to their self-esteem, it helps children learn how to wait for a turn.

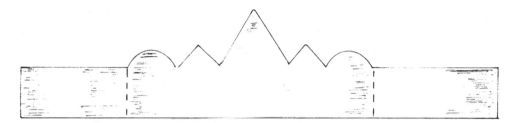

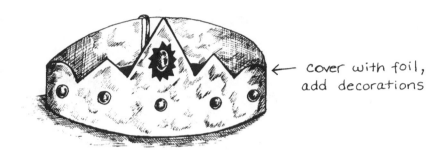

← cover with foil, add decorations

Words to use

helper
crown

wait for a turn
responsible

Materials

cardboard
scissors
glitter or sequins

aluminum foil
glue
large paper clips

What to do

1. Cut out two cardboard crowns approximately 22" x 3", similar to the illustration.
2. Cover the crowns with aluminum foil and decorate with glitter or sequins.
3. Adjust the crown to the child's head, then secure in place with a paper clip.
4. Using the list of children in the class, choose one child each day to be the king or queen.
5. The next child on the list is the king's or queen's helper for the day.
6. The king or queen gets to wear the crown, be the leader and run errands for the teacher.
7. The royal helper also wears a crown, is last to leave the room and is responsible for closing the door. (They are usually happy to do this as they can anticipate being the king or queen the following day.)
8. Continue down the list until each child has had a turn to be the king or queen and the helper, then begin the list again.

Want to do more?

Use hats, aprons or buttons to designate the leader, caboose or other special helpers.

★ TRANSITION TIME

Helper Can

3+

The helper assists the teacher with errands or special jobs. Children appreciate the fairness of this idea and enjoy helping the teacher.

Words to use

can
special job
name
envelope

Materials

coffee can
2" squares of paper
markers
scissors
glue
wrapping paper, wallpaper, contact paper or spray paint
envelope

What to do

1. Decorate the can with paper or spray paint.
2. Print each child's name on a 2 inch square, then put all the names in the can.
3. When there is a special job to be done, pull a child's name out of the can.
4. After this child has had a turn, put her name in the envelope.
5. When every child has been a helper, remove the names from the envelope, put them in the can and begin all over again.

Want to do more?

Pull out children's names to choose a song or book, or to choose a child to sit by you at circle time or have another special favor

★ TRANSITION TIME

SEPTEMBER

transition activities

88

Glitter Bottles

Use glitter bottles at circle time or at nap time to relax children. Children have something to hold and play with so they keep their hands to themselves.

Words to use

bottle
glitter
relax

Materials

small plastic bottles with lids
glitter
food coloring
water
duct tape or glue gun

What to do

1. Put one to two teaspoons of glitter in the bottom of the bottle.
2. Fill to the top with water, then add a few drops of food coloring.
3. Screw the top on securely. Use duct tape or a glue gun for added safety.
4. As children join the circle, give them a bottle to hold and turn.
5. When it is rest time, let children lay on their cots and have a bottle to look at.

Want to do more?

At nap time, tell children the bottles have "sleepy time dust" in them. Make an "ocean in a bottle" by filling a plastic container 2/3 with water. Add a few drops of food coloring, then fill it to the top with vegetable oil. Move the bottle slowly to make "waves." Bubble bottles can be made by filling a bottle halfway with water, then adding a squirt of detergent and a little food coloring. Glue on the top, then shake, shake, shake. Pour 1/2 cup of corn syrup in a plastic bottle, then add food coloring. Slowly move the bottle and watch the liquid coat the sides.

★ TRANSITION TIME

Games

What Color Is My Apple?

3+

This simple color identification game is fun to play in the fall when apples are in season.

Words to use

apples
color
grow

Materials

small basket or bucket
paper apples in red, yellow and green, covered with clear contact paper

What to do

1. Group the paper apples in three stacks by color and put them in your basket.
2. Talk to the children about how apples grow and about the three different colors. Show them an apple of each color, either real apples or your paper apples.
3. Tell the children that you are going to play an apple game with them and that you will be singing two apple songs.
4. Give each child an apple from the basket. Give all the children the same color. Sing the following to the tune of "Twinkle, Twinkle Little Star" as you hand out the apples.

> *"Apples on the Tree"*
>
> *Apples, apples on the tree*
> *One for you and one for me. (repeat)*

5. Have the children identify what color apple everyone is holding.
6. Sing the following to the tune of "The Farmer in the Dell" using the appropriate color.

> *"What Color Is My Apple"*
>
> *My apple is red (substitute yellow and green as necessary)*
> *My apple is red*
> *Hi ho the derry-o*
> *My apple is red.*

Want to do more?

When the children are familiar with all the colors, give them different colored apples. When singing "What Color Is My Apple," choose a color to sing about and ask only the children with that color to hold up their apples.

★ THE GIANT ENCYCLOPEDIA OF THEME ACTIVITIES

Imagination   3+

Teaches children to be creative.

Words to use

leaves
wind
float
ground

Materials

What to do

1. Everyone pretends to be leaves high in a tree.
2. A strong wind comes along and blows the leaves off the tree.
3. Pretend to float very gently down to the ground.
4. What do the leaves see as they float downward? Where do they land? Model the movement for the children.
5. When they reach the ground, ask the children to talk about what they saw on the way down and where they landed.

★ 500 FIVE MINUTE GAMES

Looking at Leaves   3+

Develops children's sorting skills.

Words to use

pointed
round
pile

Materials

leaves
basket

What to do

1. Gather a few leaves and place them in a basket.
2. Show each leaf to the children.
3. Ask them if the leaf is pointed or round.
4. Sort the leaves into two piles, pointed and round.
5. This is a good sorting game for young children.

★ 500 FIVE MINUTE GAMES

Child in the Dell   3+

This game is patterned after the traditional "Farmer in the Dell" game, substituting children's names for farmer, wife, nurse and so on. If you have more than ten to twelve children, you might consider stopping after about half the children have been selected and repeat it later that day or the next, or divide the children into two groups if another adult is available.

Words to use

names   class
circle   alone

Materials

What to do

1. The group forms a standing circle, and one child is selected to begin. This child goes to the center of the circle, and others sing while they move in a circle around her. For example:

> *Sarah in the dell,*
> *Sarah in the dell,*
> *Hi ho the dairy-o,*
> *Sarah in the dell.*

2. The song continues in its familiar manner with the named child pointing to another. For example:

> *Sarah picks Michael,*
> *Sarah picks Michael,*
> *Hi ho the dairy-o,*
> *Sarah picks Michael.*

3. As in the original song, the last child is asked to stand alone while the others return to the group.

> Tom stands alone,
> Tom stands alone,
> Hi ho the dairy-o,
> Tom stands alone.

Want to do more?

Try reversing the rules by starting with everyone clustered together in the center of what will become a circle. The first child skips around the group while the rest of the children chant. From the outside of the group, the first child points to another child. When the chant is completed, they join hands. Gradually a circle will form around the remaining children. The final verse ("stands alone") is not chanted.

Book to read

My Friend John by Charlotte Zolotow

Home connection

Prepare a short descriptive list of the children in your group, naming each child and giving addresses and phone numbers (with permission). With four year olds and older, briefly interview each child: What do you like to eat? What is your favorite toy? What do you like to watch on television? Include the replies for each child. Parents can go over this class list with their children at home.

★ THE PEACEFUL CLASSROOM

Photo/Name Match-up Game   4+

The memory strengthening activity teaches children name/letter recognition, language development and how to take turns.

Words to use

photograph
name
card
deck
match

Materials

a snapshot of each child
cardboard
clear contact paper or laminating
    materials
markers

What to do

1. Make a card with each child's picture backed by cardboard of the same size. The cardboard may be decorated with construction paper or left plain as long as all of the backs look the same.
2. Make a deck of cards using the name of each child corresponding with the photo cards. (Perhaps some children could write their own names.) The backs of these cards should also remain plain or be decorated the same way.
3. Laminate both sets of cards.
4. Before playing this game, make sure the children have had some exposure to their written names.
5. Invite a group of 2-6 children to play the Photo/Name Match-up Game.
6. Place all of the photo cards face down in rows and columns on the table.
7. Place the name cards in a deck, face down where everyone can reach them.
8. Each player, in turn, picks a name card from the deck (they may need help from the others to read the name) and then turns over a photo card, trying to match the name card. The first few tries will be difficult, but as the game goes on, the children will use their memories to match names to photos.
9. Try not to emphasize who "wins" the game, rather give praise to each child for any match made or even for reading the names or naming the photos!

Want to do more?

This game can also be played with the photos facing up to make it easier for beginners or younger children. Switch the photo cards to the deck and the name cards to table. You may also want to add last names to the deck depending on the skill level of the children.

★ THE GIANT ENCYCLOPEDIA OF THEME ACTIVITIES

Four Seasons Game   4+

This activity will increase children's awareness of the differences in the four seasons of the year.

Words to use

seasons
symbols
clue

Materials

paper plate for each child
small place marker such as a pebble

What to do

1. Divide plates into fourths and draw a simple picture in each section corresponding to a season, for example, snowflakes, flowers, sun, colored leaves.
2. Review the names of the seasons using pictures.
3. Pass out the plates and markers to the children.
4. Have the children practice positioning the markers on the various seasons.

5. Tell the children you will give them a clue and you would like them to place a marker on the corresponding seasons. Some examples include, "bare feet," "raking leaves," "picnics," "long, dark nights," "skiing," "Easter bunny," "squirrels and nuts," etc.

Want to do more?

You can write the name of each season on the plate. You could have patterns of the seasonal symbols and have the children trace, cut and glue them onto their paper plates. Have the children make up their own clues and take turns being the "teacher."

Books to read

A Book of Seasons by Alice and Martin Provensen
Caps, Hats, Socks and Mittens by Louise Borden
Seasons by David Bennett
The Year at Maple Hill Farm by Alice and Martin Provensen

★ THE GIANT ENCYCLOPEDIA OF THEME ACTIVITIES

Alfie's Feet by Shirley Hughes
Amazing Grace by Mary Hoffman
Autumn Harvest by Alvin Tresselt
Chipmunk Song by Joanne Ryder
Frederick by Leo Lionni
Hand Rhymes by Marc Brown
Here Are My Hands by Bill Martin, Jr. and John Archambault
I'm Terrific by Marjorie Weinman Sharmat
It Didn't Frighten Me by Janet L. Goss and Jerome C. Harste
Leaves by Fulvio Testa
The Little Old Lady Who Was Not Afraid of Anything by Linda Williams
Look What I Can Do by Jose Aruego
Marmalade's Yellow Leaf by Cindy Wheeler
The Mixed-Up Chameleon by Eric Carle
My Favorite Time of Year by Susan Pearson
The Seasons of Arnold's Apple Tree by Gail Gibbons
Shoes by Elizabeth Winthrop
The Tiny Seed by Eric Carle
Where Do All The Birds Go? by Tracey Lewis
The Year at Maple Hill Farm by Alice Provensen and Martin Provensen

Records, Tapes and CDs

Beall, Pamela Conn and Susan Hagen Nipp. "Head, Shoulders, Knees, and Toes" from *Wee Sing Children's Songs and Fingerplays*. Price Stern Sloan, 1979.

Lucky, Sharron. *Hokey Pokey*. Melody House.

Moore, Thomas. "Hokey Pokey Dokey" from *Singing, Moving and Learning*. Thomas Moore Records.

Moore, Thomas. "I Am Special" from *I Am Special*. Thomas Moore Records.

Moore, Thomas. "I Get Mad At My Family" from *The Family*. Thomas Moore Records.

Palmer, Hap. "Put Your Hands in the Air" from *Learning Basic Skills Through Music,* Volume I. Activity Records, 1969.

Scelsa, Greg and Steve Millang. "Hands Jive" from *We All Live Together,* Vol. 4. Youngheart Records, 1979.

Scelsa, Steve and Greg Millang. "Sing a Happy Song" from *We All Live Together,* Vol. 3. Youngheart Records, Inc., 1979.

Stewart, Georgianna Liccione. *Toes Up, Toes Down*. Kimbo.

Weissman, Jackie. "I'm So Mad I Could Scream" from *Miss Jackie and Her Friends Sing About Peanut Butter, Tarzan and Roosters*. Miss Jackie, 1981.

"Count My Fingers" from *Songs About Me*. Kimbo.

"Head, Shoulders, Knees and Toes" from *It's Toddler Time*. Kimbo, 1982.

Finger Play and Hand Exercises. Kimbo.

Put Your Finger in the Air. Kimbo.

OCTOBER

Fall

Fingerplays, Poems and Songs

Wiggle Them

(Wiggle fingers as directed in the poem.)
Wiggle them, wiggle them,
Wiggle them so.
Wiggle them high,
Wiggle them low.
Wiggle to the left.
Wiggle to the right.
Wiggle them, wiggle them,
Out of sight.
Clap them... (clap hands)
Roll them... (roll hands around)
Snap them... (snap fingers)
End with an "opera clap," just tapping index
    fingers lightly together.

★ TRANSITION TIME

The Hammer Song

Jenny works with one hammer,
One hammer, one hammer.
Jenny works with one hammer.
Then she works with two.

Jenny works with two hammers,
Two hammers, two hammers.
Jenny works with two hammers.
Then she works with three.

Jenny works with three hammers,
Three hammers, three hammers.
Jenny works with three hammers.
Then she works with four.

Five Little Pumpkins

Five little pumpkins sitting on a gate. (hold up five
    fingers)
The first one said, "Oh my, it's getting late." (hold
    up index finger)
The second one said, "There are witches in the
    air." (hold up second finger)
The third one said, "But we don't care." (hold up
    third finger)
The fourth one said, "I'm ready for some fun."
    (hold up ring finger)
The fifth one said, "Let's run and run and run."
    (hold up pinky)
Then wooooooo went the wind.
And out went the light. (clap hands)
And the five little pumpkins rolled out of sight!
    (roll hands over each other)

This Little Pig

This little pig went to market,
This little pig stayed home,
This little pig had roast beef,
This little pig had none.
And this little pig cried,
"Wee, wee, wee," all the way home.

★ ONE POTATO, TWO POTATO, THREE POTATO, FOUR

Little Arabella Stiller

Little Arabella Stiller found a woolly caterpillar.
First it crawled up on her mother,
Then up on her baby brother.
All said, "Arabella Stiller, take away that caterpillar."

★ ONE POTATO, TWO POTATO, THREE POTATO, FOUR

The Farmer in the Dell

The farmer in the dell,
The farmer in the dell,
Hi, ho, the derry-o,
The farmer in the dell.

The farmer takes a wife....
The wife takes a child....
The child takes a nurse....
The nurse takes a dog....
The dog takes a cat....
The cat takes a mouse....
The mouse takes the cheese....
The cheese stands alone....

★ WHERE IS THUMBKIN?

Gray Squirrel

Gray squirrel, gray squirrel,
Swish your bushy tail.
Gray squirrel, gray squirrel,
Swish your bushy tail.
Wrinkle up your funny nose.
Hold an acorn in your toes.
Gray squirrel, gray squirrel,
Swish your bushy tail.

★ WHERE IS THUMBKIN?

Old MacDonald Had a Farm

Old MacDonald had a farm,
 E—I—E—I—O.
And on his farm he had some cows,
 E—I—E—I—O.
With a moo-moo here and a moo-
 moo there,
Here a moo, there a moo, everywhere a
 moo-moo.
Old MacDonald had a farm,
 E—I—E—I—O.

Continue with other animals:
Sheep...baa-baa....
Pigs...oink-oink....

Ducks...quack-quack....
Horses...neigh-neigh....
Donkeys...hee-haw....
Chickens...chick-chick...etc.

★ WHERE IS THUMBKIN?

The Old Gray Mare

Oh, the old gray mare, she
Ain't what she used to be,
Ain't what she used to be,
Ain't what she used to be.
Oh, the old gray mare, she
Ain't what she used to be,
Many long years ago.

Chorus:
Many long years ago,
Many long years ago,
The old gray mare, she
Ain't what she used to be,
Many long years ago.

Oh, the old gray mare, she
Kicked on the whiffletree,
Kicked on the whiffletree,
Kicked on the whiffletree.
Oh, the old gray mare, she
Kicked on the whiffletree,
Many long years ago.
(Chorus)

★ WHERE IS THUMBKIN?

October Learning Centers

Block Center

While children play in the Block Center they learn:

1. To problem solve as they construct with blocks.
2. To expand their expressive language as they talk about building and constructing.
3. To cooperate and to accept the work of others.
4. To organize their world using symbolic representations in block play.

Suggested Props for the Block Center

set of unit blocks (including ramps, cylinders, curves and intersections)

large wooden hollow blocks

foam blocks or waffle blocks

materials that encourage dramatic play

miniature multicultural people (men, women and children)

miniature animals from farms, zoo and forest

miniature transportation vehicles (cars, trucks, boats, airplanes and buses)

traffic signs

wheelbarrow, large toy truck, wagon

mechanical devices such as pulley, incline, wheels

a large piece of carpet (to cover the Block Center floor; to absorb the sounds of the building process and the demolition of the structures)

Curriculum Connections

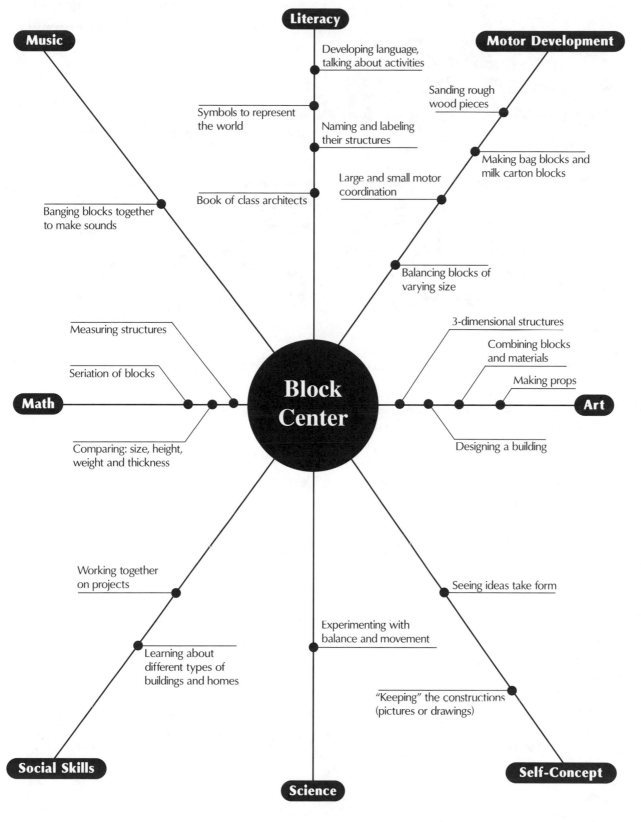

Literacy
- Developing language, talking about activities
- Symbols to represent the world
- Naming and labeling their structures
- Book of class architects

Music
- Banging blocks together to make sounds

Motor Development
- Sanding rough wood pieces
- Making bag blocks and milk carton blocks
- Large and small motor coordination
- Balancing blocks of varying size

Math
- Measuring structures
- Seriation of blocks
- Comparing: size, height, weight and thickness

Block Center

Art
- 3-dimensional structures
- Combining blocks and materials
- Making props
- Designing a building

Social Skills
- Working together on projects
- Learning about different types of buildings and homes

Science
- Experimenting with balance and movement

Self-Concept
- Seeing ideas take form
- "Keeping" the constructions (pictures or drawings)

★ THE COMPLETE LEARNING CENTER BOOK

Science and Nature Center

While playing in the Science and Nature Center children learn:

1. About the natural environment.
2. To experiment and record their ideas.
3. To develop problem solving and questioning skills.
4. To value and use methods of scientific inquiry.

Suggested Props for the Science and Nature Center

large magnifying glass
gloves
tweezers
aquarium (for fish or for growing plants)
class pet (guinea pig, white mouse or hamsters)
clear plastic jars with lids
boxes for display
sponges
balance scale
measuring tools, cups, spoons
unbreakable mirror
plastic tubs
large colander
chart paper and markers
plastic tubing
funnels
eyedroppers

Curriculum Connections

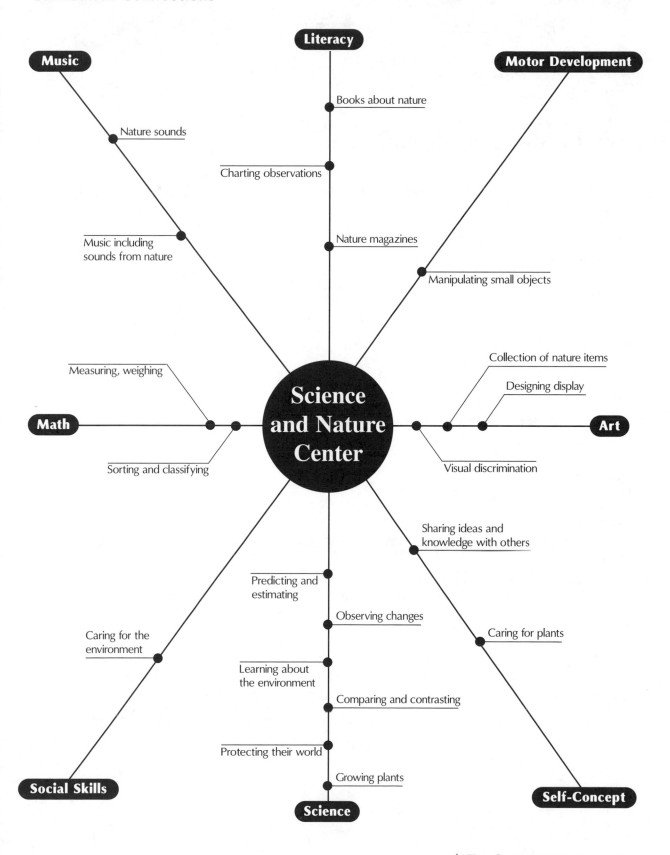

Music
Nature sounds
Music including sounds from nature

Literacy
Books about nature
Charting observations
Nature magazines

Motor Development
Manipulating small objects

Math
Measuring, weighing
Sorting and classifying

Science and Nature Center

Collection of nature items
Designing display
Art
Visual discrimination

Sharing ideas and knowledge with others
Caring for plants

Caring for the environment

Predicting and estimating
Observing changes
Learning about the environment
Comparing and contrasting
Protecting their world
Growing plants

Social Skills

Science

Self-Concept

★ THE COMPLETE LEARNING CENTER BOOK

Art Activities

Sponge Painting with Fall Colors

3+

Teaches how to use a printing technique to show trees with fall colors.

Words to use

cut
sponge
scrap
print

Materials

red, orange, yellow and green tempera paints
scissors
sponges
margarine tubs and lids
construction paper or manila paper

What to do

1. Cut the sponges into small pieces, about two inches.
2. Pour each color paint into its own margarine tub.
3. Place the lid to the margarine tub beside each tub of paint and place the piece of sponge on the lid.
4. Using scraps of paper, let the children experiment with the sponge printing.
5. Ask the children to draw a fall scene and to decorate it with their sponge paints.

Want to do more?

Encourage the younger children to experiment with overlapping the sponge prints. The older children will think of a variety of ways to use the fall sponge painting, to look like leaves on a tree beside a house, leaves that have fallen onto the ground or fall foliage seen from a distance.

★ MORE STORY S-T-R-E-T-C-H-E-R-S

Leaf Bookmark

Children develop an awareness of nature and improve fine motor skills.

Words to use

nature   leaves
contact paper   bookmark

Materials

construction paper   contact paper
leaves   scissors

What to do

1. Cut construction paper into strips 3 inches wide and 6 to 8 inches long.
2. Collect leaves on a nature walk.
3. Place the contact paper on the table sticky side up.
4. The children arrange the leaves on the contact paper. They choose a strip of construction paper to lay over the leaves.
5. They cut around the edges of the construction paper.
6. The bookmark is ready for use.

Want to do more?

You can use the same process to make place mats to be used at home or in the classroom.

★ THE GIANT ENCYCLOPEDIA OF THEME ACTIVITIES

Leaf Banners

3+

Capture a bit of fall and make a beautiful banner that the children can display.

Words to use

splatter   scrape
banner   branch

Materials

covered work table
natural colored cotton muslin cut into 8" squares (using pinking shears to prevent unraveling)
several well-formed leaves
pen
old toothbrushes
jar lids
red, yellow and brown non-toxic tempera paints
tacks or stapler
yarn, string or embroidery floss

What to do

1. Let two or three children work on their banners at one time.
2. Write the child's name in the bottom corner on the back of the cloth.
3. The children place a leaf on the muslin and splatter paint around the edge of the leaf by dipping a toothbrush in paint and scraping it over the edge of a jar lid.
4. Being careful not to move the leaf, splatter paint all the way around the leaf, then lift it up and see the imprint left behind.
5. Attach the banner to the branch with tacks or staples. Tie a piece of string to each end of the branch.
6. Allow to dry and use as is, or repeat the above steps the next day on the other side to make a double-sided banner.

Note: Oil cloth (often made of vinyl today) is a protective table covering than can be wiped clean and reused. Non-toxic tempera paints are water-based and are generally felt to be safe for use with children. They are available in art and school supply stores. Look for the AP (Approved Product) and CP (Certified Product) non-toxic seals on the labels. These are products that have been evaluated by the Arts and Crafts Materials Institute.

★ EARTHWAYS

Nasty Faces

3+

Teaches creativity and helps children work through their fears about monsters and dragons.

Words to use

monster
dragon
create
imagine

Materials

large paper plates, one per child
collage materials—ribbon, paper grass, Styrofoam pieces, tissue paper scraps, construction paper scraps, glitter
books about monsters or dragons

What to do

1. Have the books about monsters and dragons out for the children to look at.
2. Ask the children to create a monster face using the materials available.

★ THEMESTORMING

Nature Garden

Make a sculpture of natural materials.

Words to use

playdough
design
seeds
plants
dried

Materials

playdough
heavy paper plate
fall seeds and weeds such as twigs,
    nuts, thistles, pine cones, seed
    pods, leaves, rocks, fresh or dried
    flowers

What to do

1. Place a ball of playdough in the center of the paper plate. Spread the playdough out to the sides. Add more playdough to fill the plate completely with a thick layer.
2. Stick leaves, flowers and other found objects from outdoors into the playdough to make a "garden." Some leaves or weeds can also lie flat in the playdough.
3. When the design is complete, place it in the center of a table or on a shelf to enjoy.

Want to do more?

Make a miniature garden in an egg carton cup or a small paper plate. Add small figures or toys to the garden. Add a small mirror to the garden and partially bury it with playdough to simulate a pond.

★ PRESCHOOL ART

Goat Masks

4+

Here's a simple craft project that allows children to practice fine motor skills while making a goat mask. Similar techniques can be used to create other farm animal masks; the class could even perform the "Old MacDonald" song as a musical grand finale.

Words to use

goat	nose
eyes	mouth
beard	horns

Materials

large paper plate—one per mask
cotton balls
non-toxic black markers or black crayons
scissors
stapler
glue or glue stick
string or elastic cord
hole punch

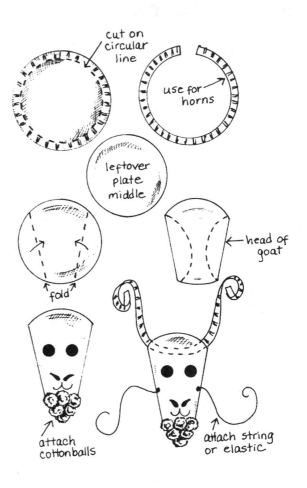

What to do

1. Have the children cut off the outer rim of the paper plate. Save this ring. It will become the goat's horns.
2. Using the inner portion of the plate, fold in the two sides to make the goat's head (see illustration).
3. Draw eyes, nose and mouth with the crayons or markers. Older children can do this themselves, but provide a model to guide them.
4. Glue two or three cotton balls on the chin to make a little beard. Stretch and fluff them out a bit with your fingers.
5. Staple or glue the outer rim of the plate on top of the head to make the horns. The tips of the horns can be curled if you like by wrapping them around your finger before attaching.
6. Cut out the eyes using a hole punch or the sharp scissors point. Make a hole on the far sides of the mask to attach the cross-string or elastic cord.

Want to do more?

Cow masks can be made by using the same technique and materials but use the whole inner circle for the cow's head—do not fold in the sides. Attach the cut rim "horns" at the top but do not curl them. Finish by painting them with appropriate colors. If you are acting out the song, the cows could wear bells around their necks.

Note: Young children are sometimes frightened by masks so introduce them carefully.

★ THE GIANT ENCYCLOPEDIA OF THEME ACTIVITIES

Pumpkin Face Mystery

4+

Teaches thinking and observation skills, along with just plain fun!

Words to use

mouth
eyes
nose
orange
black
mystery

Materials

scrap black paper
box or bucket
orange paper
glue or tape
scissors

What to do

1. Cut black paper into strange or realistic shapes to suggest a mouth, eyes, nose or other facial feature. Shapes can be very large or very small. Place these black scrap features into a box or bucket.
2. Cut orange paper into circles and ovals of all sizes ranging from very large to very small. Place a few orange circles or ovals on the floor.
3. Reach into the box and pull out a black scrap. Place the scrap on the circle or oval to begin building a face for a pumpkin. Features can be silly, realistic, scary or any style desired. The fun of this project is the mystery of how the pumpkin face will turn out, since it is created by drawing the features randomly from a box.
4. Make several different pumpkin faces. Play by changing the features around to see what different expressions and personalities can be created.
5. If desired, tape or glue the features in place and hang the completed pumpkin faces in a window, on a wall or as a doorway decoration.

Teaching tips

Some artists will choose to create random designs instead of pumpkin faces. Allow for creativity and imagination.

★ PRESCHOOL ART

OCTOBER

art activities

Spider Web

4+

Develops fine motor skills, coordination and creative thinking.

Words to use

hammer
nail
chalk
snap
cross
spider web

Materials

square of plywood, about 3′ square
pencils, crayons and felt pens
several nails
hammer
heavy string
chalk
paper
masking tape

What to do

1. With adult help, hammer a nail near the top of the plywood square. Be careful not to hammer through the wood into the floor or table.
2. Tie one end of a two to three foot piece of heavy string to the nail.
3. Place a sheet of paper in the center of the board.
4. Rub chalk back and forth on the string until the string is coated.
5. Hold the loose end of the string with one hand and pull it very tight over the paper. Use the other hand to lift the center of the string, then let go, snapping it against the paper. A puff of chalk will snap against the paper and leave a soft line.
6. Turn the paper. Rub more chalk on the string. Snap it to release another line that crosses the first.
7. Continue turning the paper and snapping chalk lines until the design begins to resemble the framework of a spider web.
8. When ready, move the paper to a table and add the connecting spider web lines with chalk, pencil, felt pen or crayon. Add a spider too, if desired.

Teaching tips

White chalk on black paper is effective as are a variety of colors on white or black paper. When the chalk sticks are rubbed back and forth, the string scores the chalk and the stick breaks easily. Use these small pieces to continue rubbing the string. When pieces are too small to handle, save them for other art activities where chalk is crushed or grated. Keep in mind that some artists will create a design instead of a spider web.

★ PRESCHOOL ART

OCTOBER

art activities

Weave-a-Web

Sometimes it's fun to make something really big!

Words to use

web
weave

Materials

thumbtacks, nails or brads
string or yarn

What to do

1. Secure thumbtacks or small nails or brads in a bulletin board.
2. Encourage the children to use the string or yarn to weave a big web on the wall or bulletin board.

★ THEMESTORMING

Big Spooky House

4+

Teaches children how to design a large project with windows and doors that open and close.

Words to use

cardboard   panel
spooky   Halloween
open   close

Materials

large cardboard panel
knife and scissors
tempera paint and paintbrushes
paper
crayons
masking tape

What to do

1. With adult help, cut the cardboard panel to look like a roof shape at the top. Under the direction of the artist, cut as many doors and windows as desired. Leave one side of the openings "hinged" so doors and windows will open and shut or cut a "capital I" shape so the openings open from the center and fold back.

2. Place the panel flat on the floor and paint the house to have boards, bricks, shutters, shingles and other details. Dry completely.
3. Make spooky drawings on paper large enough to fit over the window and door openings. Draw ghosts, bats, pumpkins, trick-or-treaters and other Halloween images.
4. Tape the pictures over the openings from the back so the tape doesn't show.
5. Lean the spooky house panel up against a wall or door where it can be secured to stand on its own with tape or some other method.
6. Enjoy opening and closing the spooky doors and windows.

Want to do more?

Instead of a spooky Halloween theme, design a house, tree or vehicle with other types of characters inside. Some suggestions include forest creatures, storybook characters or aliens from another planet.

Teaching tips

Be prepared for some screams of delight. Make smaller spooky houses with construction paper or smaller pieces of cardboard.

★ PRESCHOOL ART

Papier-mâché Masks   5+

Children use their imaginations and fine motor skills to make masks.

Words to use

mask
papier-mâché
decorate

Materials

balloons
papier-mâché paste
newspaper
pin
paint
paintbrushes
paper towels
decorating materials (beads, wool, yarn, etc.)

What to do

1. Blow up enough balloons so every child in the class will have one.
2. Purchase or make (from flour and water) the papier-mâché paste. Wallpaper paste works well.

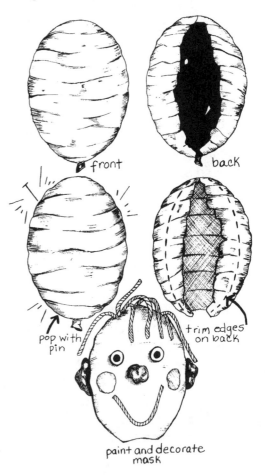

front

back

pop with pin

trim edges on back

paint and decorate mask

3. Have the children cut or tear strips of newspaper, dip the strips in the paste and put them on the balloons, about 3/4 of the way around.
4. Let the balloons dry for 24 to 48 hours.
5. When completely dry, pop the balloons with a pin and cut the hardened papier-mâché around the edges until it is shaped like a mask.
6. Explain that if children want to create faces, they can add a nose, lips, chin, etc., by taking paper towels, soaking them in papier-mâché and molding features on the face (like working with clay). Newspaper dipped in papier-mâché combined with strips of dry paper towels will facilitate the drying process.
7. Decorate the masks with paint, beads, wool, yarn, etc.

Want to do more?

Attach string or elastic to the back of the masks so the children can wear them. (Always be sure the children can see properly out of the masks.) Display the masks by hanging them on the walls of the classroom. Have children write or dictate a story about the masks they just made. Make theme masks such as farm animal masks or masks decorated with materials in one color.

★ THE GIANT ENCYCLOPEDIA OF THEME ACTIVITIES

Stocking Mask   5+

Develops creativity and fine motor skills and helps children overcome their fears.

Words to use

hanger
mirror
stocking

Materials

nylon stocking or panty hose
wire coat hanger
ribbon or rubber band
fabric scraps, rug scraps, buttons, yarn, paper clips, beads, old jewelry or earrings to make the face
glue or needle and thread

What to do

1. An adult helps the child round out a wire coat hanger with the hook at the base, to resemble the shape of a hand mirror.
2. Cut the stocking as shown in the illustration. Two masks can be made from each leg of a stocking.

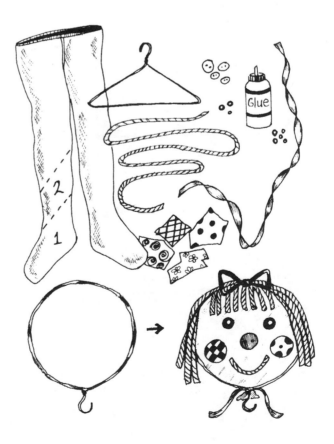

3. Pull the section of stocking with the foot attached over the coat hanger and secure with a ribbon or rubber band at the hooked end of the hanger. If the thigh section of the stocking is used, both the top and the base must be tied around the hanger.

4. Make a face on the stretched stocking with scraps, buttons, yarn or other decorative items. Glue or hand stitch the pieces on the stocking mask.

5. When dry, hold the stocking mask up to the face and speak or act while hiding behind it.

Want to do more?

If a wire hanger is not available, cut an oval of heavy cardboard into a mask shape and cut out the middle for the stocking face. This material may not be as strong as the wire hanger so the stocking may need to be cut into a single layer, stretched and stapled or taped to the cardboard.

Teaching tips

Be aware that very young children can be frightened of masks because they have not yet learned to separate fantasy and reality. Masks can make a shy child daring, a gentle child rough, a bold child quiet or a rough child gentle thereby revealing any number of secrets and surprises.

★ PRESCHOOL ART

Circle Time and Group Activities

Howdy Neighbor

3+

Use this poem to gather children for circle time or story, or to get rid of wiggles any time during the day. Children feel good when they say this poem, and they will be sitting down and listening before the poem ends!

Words to use

howdy   neighbor
clap   stomp

Materials

What to do

1. Say this rhyme and perform the motions.

> *Howdy neighbor! (make big waving motion)*
> *What do you say? (shake hands with each other)*
> *It's going to be a beautiful day. (make circle in front of body with arms)*
> *So clap your hands, (clap your hands)*
> *And stomp your feet. (stomp feet)*
> *Jump up and down, (jump)*
> *Then take a seat. (sit on the floor or in chairs)*

Want to do more?

Here's a similar poem.

> *We step, step, step (step in place)*
> *And clap, clap, clap (clap)*
> *And bow without a sound. (bow at waist)*
>
> *We step, step, step (step in place)*
> *And clap, clap, clap (clap)*
> *And then we touch the ground. (touch the floor)*
>
> *We clap down low. (clap low)*
> *We clap up high (clap high in air)*
> *We touch the ground. (touch the floor)*
> *We touch the sky. (reach hands above head)*
> *We step, step, step (step in place)*
> *And clap, clap, clap (clap)*
> *And then we sit right down. (sit down on the floor)*

★ TRANSITION TIME

I'm So Glad I Came to School

3+

Start circle time with a smile and this song. Children will review the name of their school and continue to develop a sense of belonging to the group.

Words to use

bell
school
glad

Materials

bell

What to do

1. Ring a little bell, then begin this chant.

> *I'm so glad I came to school today,*
> *I came to school today,*
> *I came to school today,*
> *I'm so glad I came to school today,*
> *I came to be with all my friends.*
> *I'm so glad I came to (name school) today,*
> *I came to (name school) today,*
> *I came to (name school) today,*
> *I'm so glad I came to (name school) today,*
> *I came to be with all my friends.*

2. Ask the children why they're happy to be at school and what they're looking forward to doing that day.

Want to do more?

Here's a song to build school identity. Sing it to the tune of "Here We Go 'Round the Mulberry Bush."

> *The name of my school is (name school), (name school), (name school).*
> *The name of my school is (name school),*
> *That's the name of my school.*
>
> *The name of my teacher is (name teacher), (name teacher), (name teacher).*
> *The name of my teacher is (name teacher),*
> *That's the name of my teacher.*

★ TRANSITION TIME

Looking Through My Window

Children enjoy using a prop to sing this name song. This activity encourages friendships and promotes positive feelings of group acceptance.

Words to use

friendship
window

Materials

empty picture frame (8″ x 12″ works well) or matte board or poster board cut to look like a window.

What to do

1. Look through the picture frame.
2. Sing the following to the tune of "Go In and Out the Window."

> *I'm looking through my window. (look through picture frame)*
> *I'm looking through my window.*
> *I'm looking through my window.*
> *And I see my friend (child's name).*

3. Pass the frame to the child whose name was mentioned in the song, then let that child look through the frame and say the name of another friend.
4. Continue until everyone has had a turn.

Want to do more?

Change the words of Bill Martin's story, *Brown Bear, Brown Bear, What Do You See?* using the children's names.

> *(First child), (first child), who do you see?*
> *I see (second child) looking at me.*

> *(Second child), (second child), who do you see?*
> *I see (third child) looking at me.*

> *After every child's name has been said, end with:*
> *Teacher, teacher, who do you see?*
> *I see all my happy children smiling at me.*

★ TRANSITION TIME

The Animals on the Farm

3+

Teaches about farm animals and the sounds they make.

Words to use

cow	dog
pig	rooster
sheep	cat
horse	chicken
duck	

Materials

small plastic and wooden farm animals or pictures of farm animals

What to do

1. Ask each child to select an animal (or picture) from the collection and then sit in a circle.
2. Start with one child. Ask her (or the group) to identify her animal and make the sound that the animal makes.
3. Sing the following song to the tune of "The Wheels on the Bus."

> *The (cow) on the farm says (moo, moo, moo; moo, moo, moo).*
> *The (cow) on the farm says (moo, moo, moo)*
> *All through the day!*

Other farm animals:

Dog	*bow, wow, wow*
Pig	*oink, oink, oink*
Rooster	*cock-a-doodle-doo*
Sheep	*baa, baa, baa*
Cat	*meow, meow, meow*
Horse	*neigh, neigh, neigh*
Chicken	*cluck, cluck, cluck*
Duck	*quack, quack, quack*

4. Repeat with the next child and her farm animal.

Want to do more?

Art: Use animals or animal masks created during an art activity as props for the song. Repeat the activity using pictures.

★ THE GIANT ENCYCLOPEDIA OF CIRCLE TIME AND GROUP ACTIVITIES

Peekaboo Farm

Teaches children about farm animals.

Words to use

identify
name

Materials

magnetic board or metal
cookie sheet
large animal cutouts with
magnetic tape on back

← expose part of animal slowly from behind board

① Animal cut out with magnetic tape on back

magnetic board or metal cookie sheet

② process repeats till all animals are on front of board

What to do

1. The teacher sings "Old MacDonald's Farm" while holding the magnetic board. The animal cutouts are attached to the back of the board.
2. During the part of the song, "...and on his farm, he had a _____," the teacher very slowly exposes part of the animal picture or cutout from behind the board.
3. The children are encouraged to identify the animal as soon as they can and to sing about that animal in the song. Place the animal on the front of the board once it is identified.
4. At the same part in the next verse of the song, the process repeats until all animals are on the front of the magnetic board.

Note: The slow process of exposing the animals should take place at different points on the board (side, top, corner, bottom). Show different parts of the animals (tail of the pig, wing of the bird, foot of the cat).

Want to do more?

Science: After all animals are on front of the board, point to one animal and ask the children to respond with the appropriate sound the animal makes.

Music and movement: Ask children, "Do we know a song about a _____?" and point to one of the animals on the board. Sing that song. This game could be played with cutouts of other items such as transportation vehicles, zoo animals, community helpers.

Math: Sort or classify the animals into various groups, such as animals that have feathers, animals that eat hay.

Books to read

Barn Dance by Bill Martin, Jr.
Early Morning in the Barn by Nancy Tafuri
Good Morning, Chick by Mirra Ginsburg
I Went Walking by Sue Williams
Old MacDonald Had a Farm by Tracey C. Pearson
Sheep in a Jeep by Nancy Shaw
The Big Red Barn by Margaret Wise Brown
Who Took Farmer's Hat? by Joan L. Nodset

Songs to sing

"Boogie Woogie Piggie"
"Mary Had a Little Lamb"
"Old Lady Leary's Cow"
"Three Little Ducks"

★ THE GIANT ENCYCLOPEDIA OF CIRCLE TIME AND GROUP ACTIVITIES

Apples and Pumpkins   3+

Teaches children about farms and harvesting during fall.

Words to use

apples
pumpkins
farm
harvest

Materials

Apples and Pumpkins by Anne Rockwell

What to do

1. Show the children the cover of *Apples and Pumpkins* and discuss that this is a book about a farm, the Comstock farm, and a little girl who went with her family to the farm and helped with the harvest.
2. Read *Apples and Pumpkins,* and at the end ask the children how the little girl helped with the harvest.
3. Encourage the children to tell about farms they have visited, or if they live on farms, have them talk about the crops they harvest.
4. Since the book is a short one, read it a second time, then dismiss the children from the circle by asking them which they like to eat, apple pie or pumpkin pie.

★ MORE STORY S-T-R-E-T-C-H-E-R-S

Autumn Book

Children create a book for the classroom that is made up of drawings made by the children and objects they collected from outside.

Words to use

fall
autumn
observation

Materials

white paper
crayons
felt pens
clear contact paper
yarn
hole punch
tape
paper bags

What to do

1. Take the children outside to search for autumn things to go in the classroom's Autumn Book. Autumn things can be leaves, flowers, ferns, twigs or small rocks.
2. Encourage them to notice what the autumn day looks like. While outside ask questions such as: Is the sky blue or cloudy? Is the grass wet or dry? Is it chilly or warm?
3. Back in the classroom have each child draw a picture of what they have just observed. Write the children's names on each paper. Cover both sides of the pictures with contact paper.
4. Choose an autumn object from each child's collection and cover these with contact paper. Punch holes along the edge of all the autumn pictures and objects and tie them together with yarn to create a classroom Autumn Book.
5. Keep this book in the classroom throughout the year. The children will enjoy seeing their artwork and remembering that special autumn day.

Want to do more?

Make a classroom book for each season. It is an enjoyable way to compare seasonal objects and the different interpretations of each season.

★ THE LEARNING CIRCLE

OCTOBER

circle time activities

The Alphabet Ghost

3+

A seasonal approach to learning about letters.

Words to use

letters
ghost
hide

Materials

white poster board
scissors
broad-tip marker

What to do

1. Prepare large alphabet flashcards with the poster board. Draw the letters with broad-tip markers. Learn the Alphabet Ghost Song.
2. With young children begin with three to five flashcards face up on the floor.
3. Ask the children to study the letters
4. After a short time turn the cards face down.
5. Choose a Ghost. The Ghost takes away one letter and hides it behind his or her back at the appropriate time in the song.
6. Sing the Alphabet Ghost Song to the tune of "Twinkle, Twinkle, Little Star."

> *The ghost flies in right through the door*
> *And hunts for letters on the floor.*
> *He grabs them quick and hides them well.*
> *Where he hides them, he won't tell.*
> *Off he goes to wait some more*
> *For letters lying on the floor.*

7. Turn the letters face up and see who can guess the missing letter.

★ THE LEARNING CIRCLE

Halloween—Witch's Brew

Teaches children cooperation and how to take turns.

Words to use

cauldron
ingredients
brew

Materials

large pot (cauldron)
large spoon for stirring
milk (1 1/2 cups)
vanilla (2 teaspoons)
orange juice concentrate (12-ounce can)
water (1 1/2 cups)
ladle
cups

What to do

1. Talk about the witch's brew and how the children together will make a lucky witch's brew.
2. The children take turns putting the ingredients in the cauldron and stirring. (With older children, you may want to ask the children to pretend to be witches and have the ingredients represent items associated with Halloween, for example, the orange juice concentrate could be pumpkin guts; the milk could be juice from a milkweed plant, etc.)
3. Ladle the witch's brew into a cup for each child.

Want to do more?

Art: Make and wear witch hats made from construction paper.

Original song
> "The Witch's Brew Song"
>
> *Stirring and stirring and stirring our brew*
> *Ooooo-ooooo-ooooo-ooooo-ooooo*
> *Stirring and stirring and stirring our brew*
> *Ooooo-ooooo-ooooo-ooooo-ooooo*

Book to read

Candy Witch, by Steven Krol

★ THE GIANT ENCYCLOPEDIA OF CIRCLE TIME AND GROUP ACTIVITIES

Jack-o-Happy

3+

Teaches children how to identify different feelings.

Words to use

happy
sad
sleepy
mad
face

Materials

14 paper plates
scissors
white glue
stapler, optional
7 orange circles cut from construction paper
black marker
7 tongue depressors

What to do

1. To prepare for the activity, the teacher (with help from the children) cuts seven orange construction paper circles to fit on the paper plates. Cut the seventh circle much smaller than the rest.
2. Draw seven jack-o-lantern faces with the black marker, one on each orange circle. Draw the faces to be: happy, sad, sleepy, mad, puzzle pieces, small, pie (see illustration).
3. Glue each orange circle to a paper plate. You will have seven plates with circles and seven plates left over.
4. Next, glue a tongue depressor to the back of each of the plates with orange circles (see illustration). Staple the tongue depressor to the plate for extra strength, if desired. Dry completely.

5. Glue or staple another paper plate to the back of the first seven plates with orange circles, covering the end of the tongue depressor like a sandwich. This gives the plates extra strength for heavy use by children.
6. On the back of each plate print the word that corresponds to the orange jack-o-lantern face: happy, sad, mad, pieces, small, pie.
7. At circle time say the following poem, reciting the words and holding up the pumpkin faces in front of your face. Use voices that match the type of pumpkin you are holding, such as bright happy voice, sad almost crying voice, sleepy yawning voice, growling mad voice, broken staccato voice, teeny tiny squeaky high voice and a normal very proud voice for the pie.

> *"Jack-o-Happy"*
> *I am Jack-o-Happy*
> *I am Jack-o-Sad*
> *I am Jack-o-Sleepy*
> *I am Jack-o-Mad.*
> *I am Jack-o-Pieces*
> *I am Jack-o-Small*
> *I am Jack-o-Pie*
> *The Best of Them All.*

8. Ask for volunteers to hold the jack-o-faces. Give one pumpkin face to each of seven children. All the children can say the poem together changing their voices with each line or the child holding the specific pumpkin face may say her line alone as her turn comes up in the poem.

Want to do more?

Language: One child may wish to dramatize the Jack-o-Happy poem for the entire group. Children love to make their own characters, voices and dramatizations. Other jack-o-faces could include: Jack-o-Kitty, Jack-o-Earth, Jack-o-Baby, Jack-o-Giggle, Jack-o-Grumpy.

Math: Make a second set of faces. Children can match the faces. Fill an egg carton with little cut-out jack-o-faces with different attributes, such as sad, happy, large, small, that the children can sort.

Books to read

Little Witch's Big Night by Deborah Hautzig
Strega Nona by Tomie dePaola
The Teeny Tiny Woman by Paul Galdone

Songs to sing

"Five Little Pumpkins Sitting on a Gate"
"Oh, Do You Know the Pumpkin Man?"
"The Witch Is on Her Broomstick"

★ THE GIANT ENCYCLOPEDIA OF CIRCLE TIME AND GROUP ACTIVITIES

Dramatic Play Activities

Leaf Crowns

3+

Leaves are an abundant and wonderful material for making crowns.

Words to use

stem
leaf
attach

Materials

lots of recently fallen
  leaves with stems
a basket to hold the
  leaves

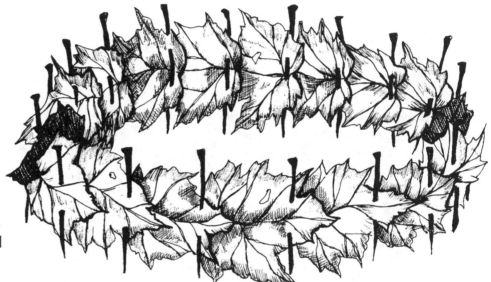

What to do

1. Spend some time gathering the leaves you will use. The children will want to help you with the gathering.
Note: Very dry, brittle leaves will disintegrate very quickly. Use fairly large, freshly fallen leaves.
2. Sit in a place where you can see the children playing and where they can see what you are doing.
3. Take two leaves and remove the stem of one at its base. Overlap the tip of one leaf and the base of the other and use the stem to attach the two leaves by pushing it down through the place where the two leaves overlap and back up again, like a straight pin.
4. Continue to attach the leaves to each other in this way. Try the crown on a child's head and when it is big enough, attach the last leaf to the first in the same way. A crown!
5. Continue to make the crowns for other children. Encourage the children's imaginative play by addressing them "in character": "Leaf Family," "Prince Fall," "Queen Autumn," etc.
6. Make leaf crowns or garlands to decorate your classroom.
7. The children join in the activity by bringing you more leaves, removing the stems or, with the older children, making their own crowns, with assistance if needed.

★ EARTHWAYS

Prop Boxes

3+

Children develop language skills, coordination and social skills when playing with prop boxes.

Words to use

trees	houses
cars	trucks
animals	

Materials

collection of farm animals	plastic trees and houses
zoo animals	small cars and trucks
collection of small animals	

What to do

1. The addition of a box of props encourages children to build with blocks in new directions.
2. A collection of farm animals and farm machinery can inspire block building that is related to farm life.
3. A box of plastic trees and small houses along with miniature people encourages builders to design a city with parks and streets.

★ THE COMPLETE LEARNING CENTER BOOK

The Wizard

3+

Enhances children's imagination.

Words to use

wizard   imagine

Materials

What to do

1. Choose a child to be the wizard.
2. The wizard walks around the room while everyone chants:

> *I am the wizard, the wonderful wizard,*
> *Alakazaam, kazoo.*
> *I am the wizard, the wonderful wizard,*
> *And now I turn to YOU.*

3. At this point, the wizard taps someone on the head and says, "You are a ___."
4. The wizard tells this child to be whatever the wizard chooses, such as a cat, a monster, a fish, etc.
5. This child then becomes the wizard.
6. A three-pointed hat and a wand are wonderful props for this game.

★ 500 FIVE MINUTE GAMES

dramatic play activities

What's Cooking?

3+

This activity will introduce children to a variety of nutritious fall vegetables and involve them in making soup.

Words to use

ingredients   peel
vegetable names   wash
cut

Materials

Stone Soup, by Marsha Brown
crock pot
chart showing the vegetable soup recipe:
3 medium tomatoes
3 carrots
3 stalks of celery with tops
1 medium onion
3 medium potatoes
3 cups of water
1 teaspoon of salt
1 teaspoon of pepper
3 beef bouillon cubes
10 oz. package frozen peas
cutting board
measuring cup and spoons
sharp knife and table knife
peeler
large spoon

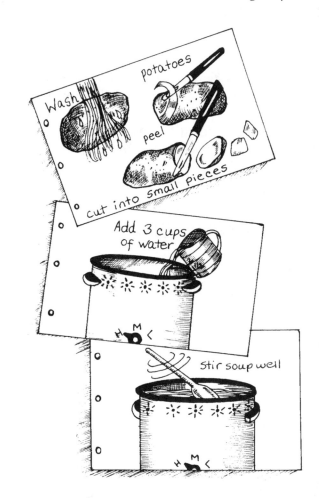

What to do

1. Assign children different ingredients to bring from home or provide them yourself. Place all the cooking ingredients and utensils on a low table so children can see and participate. Make the recipe chart and put it where it can be easily seen.
2. Read *Stone Soup* by Marcia Brown. Talk about how the soldiers in the story made their soup and how the children are going to make their soup today.

3. Ask the children to wash their hands. Allow the children to help prepare the vegetables for the soup. Good tasks for the children are washing and peeling vegetables (if peeler is not too sharp), measuring and adding ingredients, slicing the softer vegetables with a table knife and cleaning up; you should slice the harder vegetables with the sharp knife. Follow these steps, adding each vegetable to the crock pot when it is ready:
   ✓ Wash, peel and cut the tomatoes.
   ✓ Wash, peel, slice and add the carrots.
   ✓ Wash, slice and add the celery.
   ✓ Wash, peel, cut and add the onion.
   ✓ Wash, peel, cut and add the potatoes.
   ✓ Open box and add the frozen peas.
   ✓ Add the 3 cups of water.
   ✓ Add 1 teaspoon salt.
   ✓ Add 1 teaspoon pepper.
   ✓ Add 3 beef bouillon cubes.
   ✓ Stir the soup.
4. Plug in the crock pot and cook on HIGH for 4-6 hours. When the soup is ready, pour into bowls or cups and enjoy!

★ THE GIANT ENCYCLOPEDIA OF THEME ACTIVITIES

Animal Puppets

3+

Develops children's creative expression skills.

Words to use

puppets
farm
sounds

Materials

animal puppets (bought or teacher-made)

What to do

1. Encourage the children to tell the story of "Old MacDonald Had a Farm" with the puppets.
2. With young children use two or three puppets; use more puppets with older children.

Teaching tips

There are oven mitts designed to look like animals.

★ WHERE IS THUMBKIN?

Rhyming Time

3+

Encourages children to develop listening skills.

Words to use

rhyme sounds like

Materials

box of small objects

What to do

1. Read stories and poems with rhyming words.
2. Put out a box of small toy objects.
3. Ask the children to name each object.
4. When the children can correctly identify each object, ask them to find objects with names that sound alike, for example, cake, rake; boy, toy, etc.

★ THE INSTANT CURRICULUM

Writing Animal Rhymes

3+

Children will learn rhymes using the pattern in Pretend You're a Cat.

Words to use

rhymes animal names

Materials

Pretend You're a Cat by Jean Marzollo
chart tablet and markers or chalkboard and chalk

What to do

1. With a few children, read several of the animal rhymes in *Pretend You're a Cat*. Focus on the pattern the author uses of asking questions to structure the rhyme. Read the cat and squirrel rhymes.
2. Let the children choose three animals they would like to add to the book, such as a monkey, a goat and a deer.
3. Brainstorm some behaviors and movements of these animals, such as monkeys swing from trees, scurry around, climb up high, eat bananas, hold their babies, chatter, play and tease.
4. From the brainstorm list, use the pattern and write some additional rhymes. The one for the monkey might read:

> *Can you climb*
> *Up high?*
> *Nearly touching*
> *The sky?*
> *Can you swing*
> *From the trees?*
> *Can you chatter,*
> *Play and tease?*
> *What else can you do like a monkey?*
> *By Shirley Raines*

Teaching tips

Young children can brainstorm ideas for you to write the animal rhymes. Older children can pair up and write them together. Add artwork to the poems and create a classroom book about animals.

★ More Story S-t-r-e-t-c-h-e-r-s

Guest Spot   3+

Develops children's expressive language.

Words to use

describe   color
feel   What sound does it make?

Materials

assorted items from the classroom and home

What to do

1. Bring to class an interesting object that will stimulate descriptions, statements or questions, such as a butterfly in a box, a stuffed animal, a goldfish or gerbil in a bowl.
2. Encourage children to talk about the object. Ask open-ended questions that require more than a yes or no response.
3. Extend the children's statements. Example: If the child says, "The fish is swimming," the teacher might add, "up and down in the bowl."

★ The Instant Curriculum

On Stage   3+

Encourages the development of expressive language.

Words to use

describe
stage
perform

Materials

masking tape

What to do

1. Using masking tape, tape a rectangle shape on the floor.
2. Let children take turns standing on the "stage" and describing what they would do if they were on a real stage.

★ The Instant Curriculum

What's a Monster Look Like? 4+

Encourages the development of expressive language.

Words to use

describe
monster
scary

Materials

marker
easel and paper

What to do

1. Ask a small group of children to tell you what a monster looks like.
2. Record all responses.
3. Ask them if they are afraid of monsters and why.
4. Ask them if they like to dress up like monsters.
5. Ask them how they think monsters feel.

Want to do more?

Draw a monster according to the directions given by the children. Have the children draw their own idea of what a monster looks like. Dress up like monsters.

★ THEMESTORMING

Hot Potato Stories 4+

In order to succeed with "Hot Potato Stories," children have to link their comments with those that precede them. They have to take turns and listen patiently until they have an opportunity to contribute.

Words to use

cooperate
listen
patient
contribute
together
continue

Materials

What to do

1. Tell the children you have a cooperative game to play in which they will work together to make up their own special story. Tell them you will begin. After you tell the story for a short while, you will stop, and someone else will continue the story. Then another child will have a turn. After that child tells some of the story, someone else will keep it going, and so on until all the children have contributed to the story.

2. Once you are sure these instructions are understood, begin with the following "story stem" (or make up your own). Elaborate as you proceed, providing detail to make the story more interesting.

> *Once upon a time, a little girl and a little boy lived next door to each other and were friends. They were tired of being bossed around by all the adults. One day they decided to run away, so they gathered food into two little bags. When no one was watching, they left along a road near their homes.*
>
> *Pretty soon the road went right into a forest. "This is strange," they thought, "We didn't know there was a forest near our homes." Well, they didn't want to go back, so on they went, right into that forest. At first the air was warm, the sun sparkled down through the leaves, and they could hear beautiful bird sounds. But then the forest turned dark and cold, and scary sounds came from all around.*
>
> *The children decided to leave the forest. When they turned to go back, though, the path was gone, replaced by big rocks and thorn bushes. With every step they took, the path disappeared behind them, for this was a magic path. Well, they had nowhere to go but straight ahead.*
>
> *After a little bit, the path made a bend. They heard something coming from around that bend, something they could not see. But they could hear it coming. The two children stopped and hugged each other tightly. Then suddenly from around the bend came a ....*

At this point, invite children to keep the story going. No one should interrupt the new teller until she stops. You can repeat and ask simple questions to help the new speaker elaborate ("Oh, no! It was a dragon! What color was it? Was it nice or a mean dragon? What happened next?")

3. When you think the children are ready to end the story, pick up the story line with a prepared ending. For example:

> *Suddenly, the little girl became very tired and lay down on the forest path. She immediately fell asleep. She awoke to someone shaking her arm. "No, no, get away," she thought. Then she opened her eyes. She was in her room, and her mother was shaking her arm. "Time to wake up and go to school, Sarah." "Oh, Mommy. I had the (funniest, scariest, most exciting) dream! It was about (briefly describe)." "Wow, what a dream," her mother said. "That's for sure," replied Sarah. The end.*

Want to do more?

Invite storytellers to your class to tell short stories to the children. Perhaps they can finish with a "Hot Potato Story" of their own. Use simpler stories and take less time when telling stories to younger children.

Home connection

Children can teach their parents how to do "Hot Potato Stories" at home.

★ THE PEACEFUL CLASSROOM

Gift Giving

4+

Develops children's imagination and encourages generosity.

Words to use

gift
give
imaginary

Materials

What to do

1. Ask one child to come forward.
2. Tell this child that you are going to give him a gift.
3. Without saying a word, put an imaginary ring on his finger.
4. Ask the children if they know what the gift is.
5. Talk with the children about different gifts that they would like to receive.
6. Then ask if someone would like to give an imaginary gift to another person.
7. If they are not sure how to do it, show them.
8. This is a wonderfully creative game.

★ 500 FIVE MINUTE GAMES

Nut Sort   3+

Develops hand-eye coordination and visual discrimination skills.

Words to use

acorns
pecans
walnuts
almonds
filberts

Materials

a variety of shelled nuts (acorns, pecans, walnuts, almonds, etc.)
muffin tin

What to do

1. Ask the children to sort the nuts into the muffin pan by color, shape, size or type of nut.
2. After they have sorted the nuts by one attribute (size, color, shape, etc.) ask them if they can sort the nuts by another attribute.

★ WHERE IS THUMBKIN?

Button to Button   3+

Encourages children to observe and note differences and similarities.

Words to use

sort
same as
different from

Materials

buttons
egg carton
glue

What to do

1. Collect several different types of buttons, for example, one hole, two hole, four hole, red, white, black, blue, round, square, etc.
2. Take an egg carton and glue one button on the inside of each section of the egg carton.
3. The children sort the remaining buttons into the sections according to an established criteria, such as number of holes, color, shape, etc.

★ THE INSTANT CURRICULUM

Touch Me, Feel Me, Know Me—or Wake Up Your Fingers

3+

In this activity, children are urged to explore with their hands. They handle various items from their surroundings and identify, sort, group and classify them. In addition, their vocabulary grows as they seek the words needed to describe what they feel.

Words to use

texture	touch
feel	similar

Materials

collected items from the outdoors, such as rocks, leaves, soil, twigs, objects similar in size but different to touch
paper bags

What to do

1. Show the child two items very different in size, shape and texture. Put items in the bag. Let the child reach in and touch one object. As the object is touched and felt, the child identifies it.
2. Add more items to make four or five items in the bag. Repeat the above procedures.

Want to do more?

Language: Ask the children to look for things from outdoors or from home to use in this touching game. The children exchange bags and try to identify each other's choices. Ask the children to describe what is in their bags for others to guess.

Music and movement: Run a texture relay. The teacher names a texture. The child runs to the bag, reaches in, selects that texture and runs back. Speed and selection help to win the race.

★ HUG A TREE

Paper Patterns

3+

Teaches children to explore patterns with geometric shapes.

Words to use

circle	triangle
rectangle	patterns

Materials

colored construction paper
scissors
adding machine tape or paper cut in long strips
glue or tape

What to do

1. Cut circles, squares and triangles that are all the same color.
2. Children create patterns with the geometric shapes on adding machine tape or other horizontal strips of paper.
3. After exploring various patterning possibilities, the children glue their favorite pattern on the paper.

Want to do more?

Provide children with holiday patterns, such as pumpkins, ghosts and witches for Halloween or trees, stars and balls for Christmas. Follow the paper patterning process described above.

★ THE INSTANT CURRICULUM

And One More...

3+

Encourages children to notice math concepts in familiar stories.

Words to use

one	two
three	how many?

Materials

What to do

1. Allow the children to act out stories like *The Gingerbread Boy* and *The Big Turnip* which add characters to the story one at a time.
2. After each new character is added, ask the children, "How many people or animals are in the story now?"

★ THE INSTANT CURRICULUM

Teaches numeral recognition and counting skills.

OCTOBER

Words to use

acorn
squirrel
count

Materials

ten 6″ squirrels cut from
    construction paper
paper cups
stapler
markers
acorns

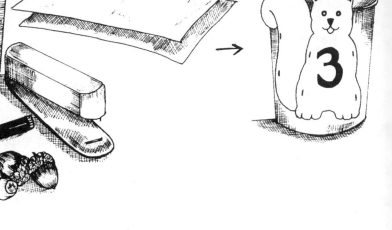

What to do

1. Staple a paper cup to
   each squirrel so the
   squirrels stand up.
2. Number the squirrels from 1 to 10.
3. The children count the appropriate number of acorns into each cup.

★ WHERE IS THUMBKIN?

Pumpkin Seriation 4+

Develops children's sequencing skills.

Words to use

small
large
in order

Materials

orange construction paper
markers
scissors

What to do

1. Cut out several pumpkins ranging in size from very small to large.
2. The children place the pumpkins in order from smallest to largest.

★ WHERE IS THUMBKIN?

math activities

Sewing a Spider's Web

Children improve their fine motor skills and practice number recognition and sequencing while sewing a spider's web.

Words to use

sew
web

Materials

cardboard rectangle or large
   meat trays (approximately
   8" x 6") with ten holes
   punched around the edges,
   one per child
black or orange yarn
childproof plastic needles
number lines from one to ten,
   as needed

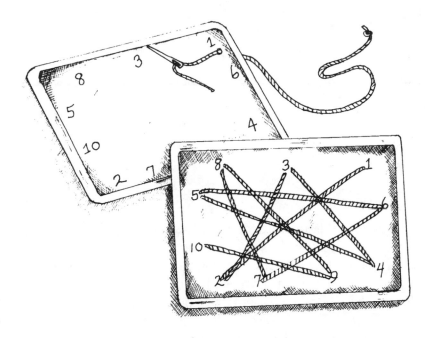

What to do

1. Around the rim of the cardboard or tray, write the numbers from one to ten out of
   sequence (see illustration).
2. Thread the needles with yarn and knot the end. If possible, have the children do this.
3. Begin the first stitch at number one (sew up from behind, so the knot will be on the back) and
   make each stitch to the next number in its proper sequence through ten. This will make the spider's
   web. Have number lines available (taped to the table or in some way displayed in the work area) for
   those who need them.

Want to do more?

Make a spider out of black construction paper and put it inside the web.

Books to read

Be Nice to the Spiders by Margaret Graham
The Very Busy Spider by Eric Carle

★ THE GIANT ENCYCLOPEDIA OF THEME ACTIVITIES

Counting Pumpkin Seeds

4+

Develops counting skills.

Words to use

seeds
numerals
plate
count

Materials

pumpkin seeds
bowl or basket
paper plates
markers

What to do

1. For younger children, write the numerals 1 through 5 on five paper plates. Also draw the same number of dots on each plate. For example, on the plate with numeral 3 draw three dots. For older children, write the numerals 1 through 10 on ten paper plates.
2. Put out the plates and a bowl filled with pumpkin seeds.
3. Ask one child to take a paper plate, count the number of dots on the plate and then count out the same number of pumpkin seeds from the bowl.
4. Continue until each child has a turn counting out the pumpkin seeds on a plate. After each child takes her turn, return the seeds to the bowl so each child can choose the plate she wants to use.
5. On another day, ask the children to fill the plates in numerical order.

Want to do more?

Art: Carve a pumpkin as a class project and ask the children to make drawings of their class jack-o-lantern.
Field trip: Visit a pumpkin patch where the children can pick their own pumpkins.
Math: Sequencing. Take pictures of the children carving a pumpkin (use an instant camera so the children can sequence the pictures of carving the pumpkin on the day it is carved).
Science: After Halloween put the jack-o-lantern in a glass terrarium so the children can observe how it decays. Record the children's descriptions of what they see. The decayed pumpkin makes excellent fertilizer for planting seeds later in the year.

Books to read

How Spider Saved Halloween by Robert Kraus
Pumpkin Moonshine by Tasha Tudor

★ THE GIANT ENCYCLOPEDIA OF CIRCLE TIME AND GROUP ACTIVITIES

Fishing Line

Teaches children matching skills in addition to numeral recognition.

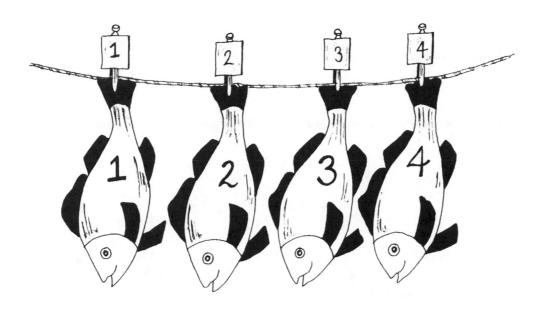

Words to use

match
numeral
fish
clothespin

Materials

yarn or clothesline
clothespins
markers
construction paper
scissors

What to do

1. Prepare a fishing line with numbered clothespins (one through ten) on it. The clothespins should be in sequential order.
2. Draw and cut out ten fish; write numerals one through ten on them.
3. Have the children place numbered fish on the line by matching the correct numerals.

★ THE INSTANT CURRICULUM

My Number Page

5+

Teaches children the value of numerals.

Words to use

numeral
correspond

Materials

construction paper
stapler
markers
stickers, stamps or cut-out magazine pictures
glue or tape

What to do

1. Fold two or three pieces of construction paper in half and staple to make a book.
2. Print "My Number Book" on the cover.
3. Write one numeral on each page of the book.
4. Allow children to paste stickers, stamps or cut-out magazine pictures on each page to correspond with the numeral on that page.

Teaching tips

With young children, put the same number of dots on each page. The child can cover each dot with a sticker or picture.

★ THE INSTANT CURRICULUM

Music and Movement Activities

Falling Leaves   3+

Children move like leaves drifting down and swirling in the wind.

Words to use

autumn
drift
swirl
sway
wind
gust
gentle

Materials

a recording of the song "Autumn Leaves" or a waltz tune
cassette tape or record player

What to do

1. Observe the ways the leaves are falling from the trees, swirling, drifting, some landing nearby and others far away.
2. Play the music "Autumn Leaves," and begin to sway. Move around the room in the way you want the children to move.
3. Then, tell the children you are the tree and they are the leaves. At first, all the leaves are attached to the tree, so they must all stand near you or touching you. Then pretend a little wind is beginning to rustle the leaves. A few leaves blow away and begin to dance on the wind. Then a large gust of wind comes along and blows most of the leaves from one side of the tree, but the others remain. Continue the slow gentle winds and the gusts of wind until all the leaves are dancing on the breeze.
4. Sway to the music with your arms outstretched. When the music stops, all the leaves are on the ground ready to be raked.

Teaching tips

Children who are reluctant to move in response to the music can be your last little leaves. Hold their arms and sway with them until the music stops.

★ STORY S-T-R-E-T-C-H-E-R-S

OCTOBER

Pass the Pumpkin ✗   3+

Teaches about musical tempo and how to take turns.

Words to use

pass
tempo
stop

Materials

pumpkin, real or plastic
drum, such as a tom-tom

What to do

1. Seat children in a circle.
2. Provide a plastic (or a real) pumpkin for children to pass while the teacher beats a tom-tom.
3. Children pass the pumpkin to the tempo of the music. Teacher alternates between slow and fast.
4. When the music stops, the child who has the pumpkin stands and takes a bow.
5. Continue until all the children have had a turn.

★ THE INSTANT CURRICULUM

Rhythmic Nursery Rhymes   3+

Shows how music and rhythm help children learn.

Words to use

repeat
rhythm
rhyme

What to do

1. Chant individual lines of nursery rhymes, putting equal emphasis on each word. Children repeat lines in same rhythm.
2. Claps could be added on specific words, such as those at the end of each line. Teacher: Ma-ry had a little lamb. Child: Ma-ry had a little lamb.
3. The rhythm can be changed to one putting emphasis on every other syllable: Ma, had, lit, lamb.

★ THE INSTANT CURRICULUM

music & movement activities

More Rhythmic Nursery Rhymes

3+

Musical accompaniment adds to the enjoyment of nursery rhymes.

Words to use

chant
tambourine
tom-tom
triangle
drum

Materials

What to do

1. Accompany chanted nursery rhymes with a tambourine, tom-tom, triangle or any other musical instrument.
2. Or alternate chanted lines between boys, girls and entire group. For example: Group: Jack and Jill went up the hill to fetch a pail of water. Boys: Jack fell down and broke his crown. Girls: And Jill came tumbling after.

★ THE INSTANT CURRICULUM

Singing Stages

3+

Encourages children to sing songs in different settings.

Words to use

stage   train
microphone   boat

Materials

masking tape
cardboard
chairs

What to do

1. Arrange different physical settings that relate to certain songs and that encourage children to sing.
2. For example, tape a rectangle on the floor and let children pretend it's a stage. Activity can be further enhanced by giving the children who want to sing a cardboard tube "microphone."
3. To sing a train song, put chairs in a long row.
4. While singing a boat song, children can sit in chairs placed in rows of two to "row the boat."

★ THE INSTANT CURRICULUM

B-I-N-G-O

3+

Bingo will entertain children of all ages. Letters, sequencing and counting skills are reinforced by adding a prop to this familiar song.

Words to use

letter
number

Materials

poster board
scissors
markers

What to do

1. Cut the poster board into five rectangles 8 1/2 x 11 inches.
2. On the front of each card print the letters, B, I, N, G, O.
3. Number the cards on the back from 1-5 and draw a picture of hands clapping beneath the number.
4. Pass out the cards to five children. Ask them to stand up in front of the other children in order from left to right,
5. After each verse is sung, one card is turned over, revealing a pair of clapping hands to indicate where to clap as the song continues.

> *There was a farmer had a dog*
> *And Bingo was his name-o.*
> *B-I-N-G-O, B-I-N-G-O, B-I-N-G-O,*
> *And Bingo was his name-o.*

6. When the second verse is sung, clap instead of saying the letter B. For the third verse, clap for B and I.
7. Continue leaving out letters and replacing them with a clap until you are clapping for all the letters.

Want to do more?

Change the words to introduce other letters of the alphabet. For example, "There was a frog who liked to hop and Jumpy was his name-o. J-U-M-P-Y," etc. Help children spell their names by singing them to this tune. "There is a boy that you all know and Derik is his name-o. D-E-R-I-K," etc.

★ TRANSITION TIME

Sticky Dancing   3+

Duct tape makes moving a whole different experience in this activity.

Words to use

sticky
stuck
step
dancing

Materials

duct tape
dancing music (fast tempo)

What to do

1. Tell the children they are going to do a sticky dance.
2. Roll a piece of duct tape (sticky side out) around your shoe to demonstrate.
3. Put the duct tape around the children's shoes.
4. Encourage the children take a few steps to get used to the feeling of the duct tape.
5. Start the music and invite the children to dance.
6. When the children are finished dancing, turn off the music and remove the duct tape.

Want to do more?

Art: Add strips of duct tape to the art area. The children can make collages by sticking scraps of paper to the duct tape that is rolled with the sticky side exposed.

★ THE GIANT ENCYCLOPEDIA OF CIRCLE TIME AND GROUP ACTIVITIES

Musical Hoops

3+

All the children need to cooperate by the end of this activity.

Words to use

hula hoop
remove
stand inside

Materials

music (fast tempo)
6-9 hula hoops

What to do

1. Explain that when the music is playing, the children may dance and move to the music. When the music stops, they need to stand inside the hula hoop.
2. Start the music.
3. Stop the music. Encourage the children to help each other find a hula hoop.
4. When everyone is standing inside a hula hoop, remove one of the hoops.
5. Repeat steps 2 and 3 until there are only three hula hoops left. This game encourages cooperation.

Want to do more?

Art: Make paper tube shakers or paper plate shakers. The teacher records the children playing their shakers and uses this music when playing the game.

Teaching tips

When doing this activity with a large number of children, increase the beginning number of hula hoops. Also increase the number left at the end to ensure the game will be safe.

★ THE GIANT ENCYCLOPEDIA OF CIRCLE TIME AND GROUP ACTIVITIES

Me and My Shadow

3+

What do shadows look like? Why do they change?

Words to use

shadow
sheet
lamp

Materials

bedsheets (white or light-colored) or a blank wall
gooseneck lamp

What to do

1. If you do not have a blank wall, hang the sheet where there is space for the children to move.
2. Place the lamp on a small table or chair so that it is shining on the sheet or wall.
3. Ask a child if he knows what his shadow looks like. Have him stand between the lamp and the wall so he can see his shadow.
4. Ask him if he can make his shadow move. What else can you make your shadow do? Can you make it bigger? Smaller? How?

Want to do more?

Use the lamp and sheet at group time after the children have had a chance to experiment with it individually. Pick out some music and have the children shadow dance. Show shadows of simple objects for the children to guess.

★ THEMESTORMING

Sound Effects

4+

Teaches how musical sounds enhance the experience of a story.

Words to use

sound effects
character
story
practice

Materials

tape recorder and blank tape
items that produce sound effects (rhythm instruments or common objects)
character necklaces (way to designate characters)

What to do

1. Choose a well known, predictable story (for example, *The Three Bears*).
2. Talk with the children about each character and ask them to choose a musical sound that will represent each character.
3. After selecting a musical sound for each character, ask the children to choose the character they want to be and to wear the corresponding necklace or other character identification.

4. Explain that as you read the story, you will signal which character's turn it will be to make the musical sound to designate that character. (For example, "My porridge is too hot" would be accompanied by the Mother Bear's music, playing tambourines; "My porridge is too cold" by Father Bear's music, playing drums; "Mine is just right" by Baby Bear's music, ringing jingle bells.) The more frequently this activity is repeated, the more proficient the children will become at anticipating their turns.

5. Read the story and ask the children to practice their parts. When the children are ready, record the story with the accompanying musical sounds. Play the recording and ask the children to listen for their parts. With the children, plan and create the musical sounds to accompany other familiar stories.

Want to do more?

Language: Record a variety of common sounds on a tape and place it in the listening area. Children can identify the sounds and write a story about what is making the sounds.

Science: Record sounds throughout the day and later play the recording for the children to guess what made the sounds in their classroom.

★ THE GIANT ENCYCLOPEDIA OF CIRCLE TIME AND GROUP ACTIVITIES

Science Activities

Grow a Sock   3+

Collecting seeds and nuts is a natural activity in the fall. However, a collector often overlooks many seeds because they are small and hard to recognize. An entertaining way to collect some hard to find seeds is to take a sock walk. Previously unnoticed seeds will be easily collected and as a bonus, one method of seed dispersal will become very obvious.

Words to use

dispersal
seed
germinate
plant names, as appropriate

Materials

long socks with fuzzy outer surfaces to
    which seeds will stick (i.e.
    adult knee socks)
cake pan

What to do

1. Dress each
   child in a
   thigh high pair
   of socks.
2. Go for a walk through
   a densely vegetated area. An
   empty lot overgrown with weeds would be excellent.
3. Return to home or class and look at the socks! Then take them off.
4. Wet the entire sock, and place it in a cake pan placed on a slant. (see illustration) Fill the lower portion of the pan with water so the sock remains wet.
5. Put the pan in a warm place and watch the seeds sprout.

Want to do more?

Take sock walks at different seasons. Which seeds are harder to remove? Do some hurt you? Can animals help seeds find new places to grow? Yes! Glue samples of seeds on cards to develop a seed collection. Repot sprouts and grow them to full size. Discuss other ways nature has of spreading seeds around (e.g. winged seeds—by wind, berry seeds—by birds).

★ Hug a Tree

Beat a Leaf

3+

Collecting fall leaves is probably one of the most common October activities, second only to cutting out pumpkins. By covering a leaf with fabric and hammering, children create a clear print of the leaf's structure along with a pretty picture.

Words to use

vein
stem
pigment
dye
color
chlorophyll
stain

Materials

a piece of plywood or particle board
pushpins
pieces of white sheet or similar material (torn into squares approximately 6" x 6")
leaves collected from a nearby tree
a small hammer

What to do

1. Place the leaf on the board and cover it with a piece of cloth. Use the pushpins to hold the cloth in place.
2. Using the hammer, pound on the leaf so that the color is driven into the sheet.
Note: Find a nice spot outside for the hammering.
3. Set the finished leaf print aside to dry.

Want to do more?

If the class has completed a number of leaf prints, sort them into piles of similar kinds. Identify by name and put together a leaf collection. Discuss why some leaves do or do not produce prints. Try flowers and leaves from house and garden plants. Try to wash the leaf prints out. Do a stain removal test by using various detergents or bleaches on material. Discuss natural dyes. Create a wall hanging, blanket or pot holder cover with these leaf beatings. For the truly ambitious, a quilted leaf print is quite lovely. Print several leaves on the same piece of fabric to make a mural. This makes a great holiday gift.

★ MUDPIES TO MAGNETS

A Wood Chip Garden

3+

An easy and inexpensive spin off from the terrarium is a wood chip garden. With a minimum of materials, children can take home part of an area visited to enjoy for a long time. We've even known a few to survive for years!

Words to use

terrarium	bark
moss	lichens
rocks	twigs

Materials

wood (branches or small limbs)
 cut in discs
moss
sand
white glue
miscellaneous twigs
fungi
rocks
dried wood

What to do

1. The wooden discs are the base for forming the garden. Any wood slabs or bark pieces will do. Unique gardens are made from wooden discs cut from logs. For this you need to use a table or band saw. Cut the discs 1/2-1 inch thick and 2-4 inches across. This step needs to be done by adult.
2. Collect moss or lichens from your area. Also collect sand (not beach sand, it's too salty and will kill the moss). River sand or sand from a construction site is best. Assorted rocks, twigs and other things may be collected for decorating the garden.
3. Spread a layer of glue on the wood disc.
4. Sprinkle a thick layer of sand on the glue. Shake off excess sand.
5. With the moss, twigs and rocks, plan the landscape of your little world.
6. Once the plan is complete, glue the items, including the moss, in place with small amounts of glue. Allow it to dry undisturbed and out of direct sunlight.
7. After several days of drying it will need to be sprayed with water to moisten the moss. The garden will stay green and grow if you continue to spray it and keep it out of direct sunlight.

Want to do more?

Build terrariums that represent other environments. Discuss the fact that moss can grow on a wooden disc because it has no root system, while plants with roots would die. Discuss the importance of roots.

★ HUG A TREE

Slime

3+

Sometimes what you see is not what you feel.

Words to use

mix
looks like
feels like

Materials

cornstarch
water
green food coloring
large bowls

What to do

1. Mix water and cornstarch in a bowl until they reach the consistency of mashed potatoes.
2. Add green food coloring.
3. Try to pick it up—it slips through your fingers!

★ THEMESTORMING

Leaf Catchers

4+

Catching leaves in containers provides lots of materials for graphs and comparisons.

Words to use

collect   count
most   more
least   fewer
compare   graph
guess

Materials

2 large leaf catchers, for example, wastebaskets, bushel baskets, boxes or bed sheets, label one red and one blue
shelf paper or adding machine tape

What to do

1. Choose a day when the leaves are falling and take the children outside to watch the leaves. Talk about how most trees lose their leaves each fall, but not all at the same time. Look at the trees in your area. Which ones are losing leaves *now*?
2. Show the children the leaf catchers. Ask them to look around and decide where to put one leaf catcher so it will catch the most leaves possible. Encourage them to explain their choices.

3. Now find a spot where you will catch the fewest leaves and put the other leaf catcher there. Often children choose a spot far from the tree for this catcher, but with the right breeze, it may collect more than the other container!

4. Leave the catchers outside long enough to collect several leaves, at least an hour, preferably longer. At the end of the time, bring them inside and compare. Which leaf catcher collected the most? The least? Were your guesses right? Make a graph to find out.

5. To graph the results, use a roll of shelf paper with a line drawn down the middle or two strips of adding machine tape. Label one side "Red leaf catcher" and the other "Blue leaf catcher." Mark off boxes so that one leaf will fit in each box (if the leaves are large, make the boxes large). Tape one leaf in each box, first those from one catcher, then those from the other. With the leaves lined up in a "bar graph" it's easy to see your results, with or without counting.

Want to do more?

Graph leaves according to type. Which tree is producing the most fallen leaves right now? Will it be the same tree next week? How many colors can your leaf catcher catch? Do more leaves fall during the day or overnight? How could you find out?

★ MUDPIES TO MAGNETS

Outdoor Hunt and Find   4+

On this outdoor scavenger hunt, children scour the yard for the objects on their list, picking and choosing to select those that are deemed most appropriate. As this selection process is going on, a constant dialogue between children and teachers can occur with the evaluation of objects being an ongoing, exciting process.

Words to use

list
find
hunt

Materials

bags
hunt lists (see suggested examples)

What to do

1. Choose a hunt from the hunt lists suggested based on what is appropriate for your children, or make lists of your own.

2. Discuss the focus of the hunt with the children, reviewing the particular vocabulary for the hunt you have chosen. For example, if you will be doing a texture hunt, talk about rough, bumpy, smooth, hard, soft, etc.

3. The children search the school yard or path for appropriate items. When they find objects, they are to bring them to you.

4. In some areas, picking living things such as leaves and flowers is not appropriate and may be illegal. If that is the case, before the search begins, a discussion about flowers and leaves and how living things should be cared for and protected is in order. In that case you may visit the site, note the object, and record its presence on your sheet.

5. You may use one hunt with all the children, or groups of children may do different hunts. The ability to accomplish the task would be the criteria. If you decide to have different groups working different hunt lists, you may need to have an adult accompany each group.

6. Upon finishing the hunt, bring the objects back and share what you have found.

Want to do more?

Classify the objects using criteria suggested by the children. Create collages from the various finds. Add to these as you go through the year. Place your finds in a mini-museum.

Suggested Hunt Lists for Outdoor Hunt and Find Walk

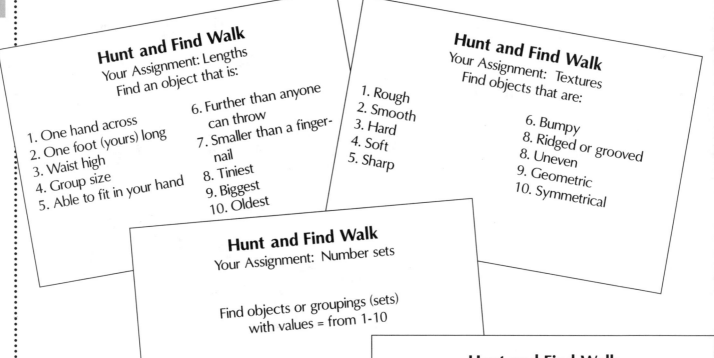

Hunt and Find Walk
Your Assignment: Lengths
Find an object that is:

1. One hand across
2. One foot (yours) long
3. Waist high
4. Group size
5. Able to fit in your hand
6. Further than anyone can throw
7. Smaller than a fingernail
8. Tiniest
9. Biggest
10. Oldest

Hunt and Find Walk
Your Assignment: Textures
Find objects that are:

1. Rough
2. Smooth
3. Hard
4. Soft
5. Sharp
6. Bumpy
8. Ridged or grooved
8. Uneven
9. Geometric
10. Symmetrical

Hunt and Find Walk
Your Assignment: Number sets

Find objects or groupings (sets) with values = from 1-10

Hunt and Find Walk
Your Assignment: Shapes
Find objects that generally are:

1. Circular
2. Triangular
3. Square
4. Rectangular
5. Heart shaped
6. Star shaped
7. Spherical
8. Cylindrical

Hunt and Find Walk
Your Assignment: Find these specific things:

1. Snail shell
2. Vine
3. A bad smell
4. A great smell
5. A flower
6. A root
7. Water
8. Over 100 years old
9. Will hold things
10. New life
11. Something useful
12. Something beautiful
13. Something you have never seen before

Hide and Seek for Critters and Kids 5+

Just as children like to play hide-and-seek in areas with lots of hiding places, animals live where there are many safe places for them. In this activity, children explore an area for their own hiding places. Then they pretend to be an animal and look for hiding places. It soon becomes obvious why even though deer like grass, they don't live in vacant lots!

Words to use

observe
examine
explore
search
record
predator

Materials

area to explore
paper and writing materials

What to do

1. Walk around the yard of your house or the playground at school with the children.
2. Observe, count and record the various places that a child might hide when playing the game hide-and-seek or kick-the-can.
3. Choose an animal. Observe, count and record the many places that that animal might hide.
4. Discuss the idea that hide-and-seek is fun for children.
5. Discuss the need for animals to have hiding places. Point out the implications if the children do not see them.
6. Compare the number of human hiding places and the number of animal hiding places.

Want to do more?

Name some favorite animals. Discuss places that they hide and why. How does the lack of hiding places affect an animal's choice of habitat? Are the animal's shape, color and texture important? What places can you hide at night that would not hide you during the day? Does a creature have to be out of sight to hide? (The answer is no. A squirrel may be safely hidden in a tree, though still in view.) How do baby animals hide?

★ HUG A TREE

Leaves Don't All Fall the Same Way   5+

Big leaves, little leaves, yellow, orange and brown leaves become as jumbled in our minds as they do in the autumn leaf piles. Millions of trees end the growing season by dropping their leaves to the ground in preparation for the winter's rest. Exploring the great variety of ways that they fall is a novel means of becoming familiar with leaves and can lead to numerous other activities such as classification and body movement.

Words to use

describe
patterns
falling leaf

Materials

paper and pencil or marker

What to do

1. Find a location under a tree where you can lie down. Choose a calm day in the fall when the leaves are falling.
2. Watch as the leaves fall naturally. A few will be falling most of the time.
3. Describe the ways that they fall. Record the descriptions.
4. If possible, shake the tree so that many leaves fall. What new fall patterns do you notice? Describe these and record them.
5. Move to an open place such as a lawn. Have each child describe and, through movement, act out a falling leaf.
6. Then, let the entire group pretend to be a forest of falling leaves.

Want to do more?

Go to different kinds of trees, see if the leaves fall in different ways. Using a rake to gather the fallen leaves, cover each child in turn (except for the head), or several children, depending on the size of the leaf pile. Describe how it feels to be a fallen leaf or to be hidden in the pile. How do fallen leaves help the forest? Discuss why leaves fall. Point out that some trees drop their leaves in fall and others do not. Do all leaves fall sooner or later?

★ HUG A TREE

Hot and Cold: Let's Get Precise

An acceptable and even recommended procedure with young children is to encourage them to develop guesses (inferences and predictions) before conducting a scientific procedure. It's good science and good learning practice.

Words to use

thermometer	hot
hotter	hottest
cool	cooler
coolest	place
sun	sunlight
shade	temperature
warm	warmer
warmest	

Materials

thermometers (4 or 5)

Note: You'll need to talk with children about thermometers. The longer the line, the hotter the temperature.

What to do

1. Take children out of doors. Observe the area around the school.
2. Ask which place they think is the hottest. Let the children choose.
3. Which place or spot do you think is the coolest? Again, let the children choose.
4. Place the thermometers on sites selected by the children, i.e., bare ground, grass, sandbox, slide, blacktop, concrete, swings, climbers, etc.
5. Wait 10 minutes. Check the thermometers and see if the children were right.
6. Which place was the hottest? the coolest?
7. Can we find some places that have the same temperature?

Want to do more?

How can you cool down a hot place? Measure something in the sun and record the temperature. Do it again when the spot is in the shade.

★ MORE MUDPIES TO MAGNETS

Tornado Tower

5+

Can such a simple thing as starting a circular motion in a liquid cause such a tremendous difference in a procedure? Yes! it can! Just try this activity without that twist and you will see the difference. The result of this twist is a tornado shaped funnel as the water moves from one bottle to another. It should be pointed out that in "real life," the tornado is the center of a low pressure area and is always moving in a counterclockwise direction in the northern hemisphere. Can you make this tornado move in both directions?

Words to use

tornado
clockwise
counterclockwise

Materials

two 16 ounce plastic soda bottles with lids
sharp knife
plastic film canister
super glue
food coloring

What to do

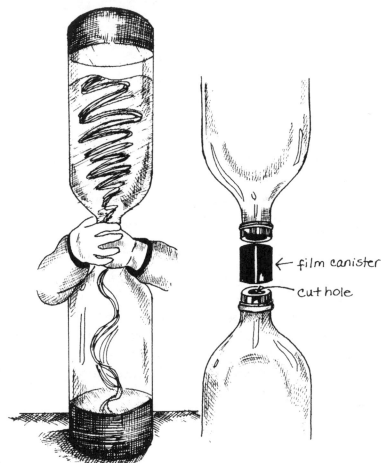

← film canister

← cut hole

1. Fill 1 bottle with water and add a few drops of food coloring.
2. With a sharp knife, cut a round hole in each of the lids. The size of the hole will determine the time it takes for the water to drain.
3. Cut the bottom from the film canister about 1/2 inch from the bottom. You will have an open tube slightly shorter than a film canister.
4. Remove the plastic rings that are left around the necks of the bottles when the lids are removed.
5. Place the 2 lids in the film canister tube so they touch each other in the center. Screw on the 2 bottles. You can make this permanent by super gluing the connection.
6. Turn to place the full bottle on top. While holding the bottles tightly, rotate the system vigorously in a counterclockwise direction.
7. A whirlpool should form in the system that resembles the tornado's shape.

★ MORE MUDPIES TO MAGNETS

What Is Hiding in the Air?

The sky is full of all sorts of things that fly. Fine particles such as smoke from burning leaves, exhaust from cars and factories, dust from fields and roads all gather in the air until gravity slowly filters them out. These particles are a part of our earth and our environment. Some will always be present, but others need not be. This activity is a good basic building block to begin to help children understand pollution and how it affects the quality of the air we breathe. That knowledge can go a long way in helping growing children make future decisions on the quality of our air.

Words to use

air pollution
airborne particles

Materials

tissues or toilet paper
pushpins or thumbtacks
4" square sheets of paper
clear petroleum jelly
tissue paper
magnifier

What to do

1. Take the children for a short walk with a box of tissues or toilet paper.
2. Select various spots on the walk to test for evidence of dirt. Choose places that appear to be clean such as picnic table tops, rail tops or large leaves of low growing shrubs or trees. Wipe across the surface of the objects. See what appears on the tissues.
3. Discuss where this material could have originated. Talk about air pollutants—dust, factory or car exhausts. They must be in the air or our tissues would not have smudged. Let's find out if we have airborne particles where we live.
4. Return to school and select 4-6 spots to run this experiment. Thumbtack down the 4" pieces of white paper at each location.
5. Cover the paper surface with a very thin layer of petroleum jelly.
6. Return to each spot daily. Remove one piece of paper each day to examine closely. Compare the amount of build up over time.

Want to do more?

Do a month long study. Check particulate count in different locations, especially near a dusty or heavily polluted spot. Read the paper and follow the news for cause and effect as it relates to your finding.

★ MORE MUDPIES TO MAGNETS

Snack and Cooking Activities

Haystacks

3+

Teaches children the concepts of measuring and change of state.

Words to use

noodles
butterscotch
melt
stir

Materials

one 6-ounce bag of butterscotch morsels
margarine
Chinese noodles
mixing spoon
electric frying pan or crock pot or hot plate and pan
wax paper

What to do

1. Melt the bag of butterscotch morsels and two tablespoons of margarine in an electric frying pan.
2. Stir in Chinese noodles.
3. Drop by spoonfuls onto wax paper and allow to cool.
4. Eat and enjoy!

★ WHERE IS THUMBKIN?

Making Butter

3+

Helps children understand the concept of cause and effect.

Words to use

cream
jar
shake
butter
change

Materials

whipping cream
baby food jars
salt
tablespoon
crackers

What to do

1. Provide each set of two children with a baby food jar.
2. Pour two tablespoons of room temperature whipping cream in each jar. (One pint of whipping cream is enough for 12 jars.)
3. Instruct the children to take turns shaking the jars until a soft ball of butter is formed.
4. Taste the butter, salted and unsalted.
5. Discuss where milk, butter and cheese come from.
6. Spread the butter on crackers and enjoy!

★ WHERE IS THUMBKIN?

Brown Bear Bread   3+

During this learning activity, children prepare bread dough and shape it into a bear for baking.

Words to use

mix
knead
dough
teddy bear

Materials

4 cups flour
1 teaspoon salt
8 teaspoons baking powder
1 teaspoon cream of tartar
2 tablespoons sugar
1 cup vegetable shortening
1 1/3 cup milk
large bowl
2 cookie sheets
pastry blender or two knives
oven
ribbon
firm paper plates
plastic bags

What to do

1. Prepare a visual recipe board (rebus chart—see page 259) with pictures and words describing the recipe step by step.
2. Purchase ingredients in the recipe and gather all utensils necessary for cooking.
4. Preheat oven to 425°F. Grease 2 cookie sheets.
5. Children need to wash their hands. Have the children help you throughout the mixing and kneading process.
6. Place flour, salt, baking powder, cream of tartar and sugar in a bowl. Cut the shortening into the flour with two knives or a pastry blender until the mixture resembles a coarse meal.
7. Add the milk all at once and stir just until the dough forms a ball around the fork.
8. Turn the dough onto a lightly floured surface and knead 14 times. Divide dough into pieces for each child.
9. Children can make their bear by dividing their dough into rolled "balls" and "snakes" and piecing together a head, two ears, a body, two legs and paws. Place the finished bear on the cookie sheet. You may also wish to add raisins for the eyes, nose, mouth and buttons.
10. Bake 15-20 minutes. Remove from oven and cool, then tie a bow around Brown Bear's neck. He will travel home better if placed on a firm paper plate before being placed in a plastic bag.

Book to read

Winnie the Pooh by A. A. Milne

Song to sing

"The Teddy Bears' Picnic," by Rosenshontz

★ THE GIANT ENCYCLOPEDIA OF THEME ACTIVITIES

Cinnamon Roll-up   3+

This activity teaches about food preparation.

Words to use

dough
flatten
roll up

Materials

refrigerator rolls found in the dairy section
butter or margarine
plastic knives
cinnamon
raisins
sugar
toaster oven

What to do

1. Separate the dough into rolls. Give each child one roll. Tell the children to unroll and flatten the dough with their fingers.
2. Ask the children to spread butter or margarine on the top of their flattened dough.
3. Put out small bowls of sugar, raisins and cinnamon. Tell the children to sprinkle all three over the butter.
4. Demonstrate how to roll up the dough so that the butter, cinnamon, raisins and sugar stay inside.
5. Bake in a toaster oven according to package directions for rolls. Let cool and serve!

Book to read

Just Me and My Dad by Mercer Mayer

★ THE GIANT ENCYCLOPEDIA OF THEME ACTIVITIES

Cream Cheese and Jelly Sandwiches   3+

Children learn to make a sandwich for snack.

Words to use

spread   bread
slice   sandwich

Materials

cream cheese
jelly
toaster
whole wheat bread
knives
napkins

What to do

1. Place the cream cheese and jelly out on the snack table until it reaches room temperature. They are easier to spread when warm.
2. With a small group of children at a time, toast the bread. Place each slice flat on a napkin.
3. Show the children how to spread the softened cream cheese on the bread. Spread the jelly on the second slice of bread.
4. Discuss with the children whether or not they like cream cheese and jelly better than peanut butter and jelly.

Teaching tips

While teachers usually serve snack to all the children at the same time, vary the routine occasionally and have a small group make their snack and enjoy it casually with you. The smaller group may prompt more social conversations.

★ STORY S-T-R-E-T-C-H-E-R-S

Pumpkin Bread

3+

Encourages children to taste a different kind of bread.

Words to use

pumpkin
banana
bread
loaf
slice

Materials

pumpkin bread
bread knife (optional)
cream cheese or margarine

What to do

1. If possible, bake the bread at the school, substituting pumpkin for bananas in a banana nut bread recipe. If not, ask a parent who is a baker to bring in an already-baked pumpkin bread.
2. Slice the bread from a whole loaf and ask the children to guess what kind of bread it might be based on its color. Some will say carrot bread or banana bread.
3. Give each child a slice and ask them to try it. Most children enjoy the taste because it is not too sweet.
4. Let children who want a spread on their pumpkin bread top it with cream cheese or margarine.

Want to do more?

If you have a microwave in your classroom, wrap the bread in a plastic wrap and heat if for just a minute or two. The aroma and the warmth will make it even more appetizing.

★ Story S-t-r-e-t-c-h-e-r-s

Baking Pies

3+

Learning how to bake encourages fine motor skills, helps children feel competent and contributes to a yummy snack!

Words to use

pie
pie shell (crust)
sliver

Materials

an unbaked pie shell (crust)
1 1/2 cups pumpkin puree
1/2 cup honey
2 teaspoons grated orange rind
1/2 teaspoon each, cinnamon and cloves
1/2 teaspoon salt
1/2 teaspoon vanilla
1/4 teaspoon each, nutmeg and ginger
2 eggs
1 cup cream or half-and-half
mixing bowl and spoon
measuring utensils
oven
plates and forks

What to do

1. Prepare an unbaked pie shell with a recipe of your choice, preferably one made with whole wheat flour.
2. In a large bowl, mix pie ingredients in the order given. Pour into pie shell.
3. Bake at 425°F for 45 minutes.
4. The recipe can be doubled to make two pies.
5. This is a very rich pie, so serve small slivers; it makes a special treat.

★ EARTHWAYS

Little Pumpkin Pies

3+

Children learn to roll pie crust.

Words to use

pie crust
dough
rolling pin
circle
crust

Materials

pie crust dough, premixed or made from scratch
rolling pin
flour
wax paper
biscuit cutter
muffin tins
shortening or vegetable oil
canned pumpkin pie filling
mixing bowl
large serving spoon
toaster oven
cookie sheet
glasses
milk

What to do

1. Turn a muffin tin over with the bottom up and lightly grease with shortening or brush with vegetable oil.
2. Demonstrate how to roll the pie crust dough by placing a sheet of wax paper on the table, lightly flouring it and rolling flat with the rolling pin.
3. Let the children roll out the dough; each child cuts one circle with the biscuit cutter.
4. Show the children how to shape their circle of crust over the individual bottoms of the muffin tins.
5. Place in a hot oven, 400°F, and brown. It only takes two or three minutes.
6. Let the tiny pie crust cool and remove from the muffin tins.
7. Precook the pumpkin pie filling so that it has already thickened. Pour into a mixing bowl. Using a large serving spoon, let the children fill their pie crusts.
8. Place the little pumpkin pies on a cookie sheet. Pop them back into the oven or microwave just long enough to warm the filling.
9. Serve at snack time with cold milk.

Teaching tips

As an alternative, if you do not have cooking facilities, bake the pie crusts at home and let children fill them with butterscotch pudding the next day.

★ MORE STORY S-T-R-E-T-C-H-E-R-S

Look Who's Here Today

3+

This chart encourages children to recognize their names and to accept responsibility.

Words to use

balloons   name
basket   find

Materials

colored construction paper
scissors
markers
hole punch
yarn
tape
push pins or stick-on tabs with hooks
basket or shallow box
bulletin board or poster board

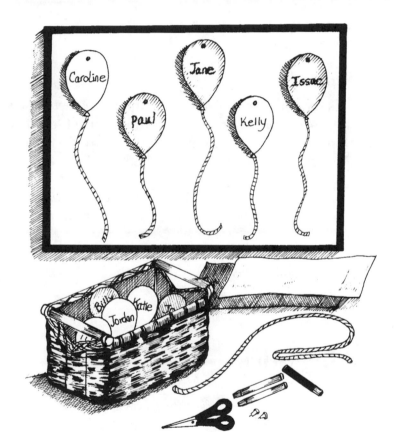

What to do

1. Cut balloon shapes out of construction paper. Write a child's name on each balloon. Punch a hole at the top, then tape a three inch piece of yarn to the bottom of each balloon.
2. Let the children hang up their balloons. Use push pins with a bulletin board, or stick-on tabs with hooks with poster board.
3. Place the children's name balloons in a basket. As they arrive in the morning, help them find their names and hang them on the board.
4. At first you will need to help the children with this, but they will quickly learn how to do it by themselves.

Want to do more?

Change name tags for seasons or monthly themes. Use apples, pumpkins, ornaments, hearts, kites, flowers, fish, etc. Envelopes or library pockets can be used in place of hooks. Make tall objects, like paper dolls or crayons, that each child can place in the envelope that has his name on it.

★ TRANSITION TIME

Musical Clues

3+

Teaches children to listen for a musical clue to know what to do.

Words to use

song
instrument
clue

Materials

recorded music
record player or tape player
musical instrument

What to do

1. For effective and enjoyable classroom management, use songs played on the record player, sung by the teacher or played on a rhythm instrument to direct children to a specific activity.

Clean up time: "Dance of the Sugar Plum Fairies" (Tchaikovsky) or "Time to Pick Up the Toys" (sung by the teacher) to the tune of "Mulberry Bush."

Now it's time to pick up the toys, pick up the toys, pick up the toys.
Now it's time to pick up the toys for all the girls and boys.

Circle time: Taps on the triangle (teacher).
Nap time: "Lullaby" (Brahms)

★ THE INSTANT CURRICULUM

Talking Stick

3+

Children learn how to take turns and listen when others are talking by using this stick.

Words to use

take turns
stick
listen

Materials

stick or dowel (12" long)
gold or silver spray paint
glue
glitter or sequins

What to do

1. Spray the stick with paint and let it dry. Decorate with glitter and sequins.
2. Show the children the talking stick and explain that only the person holding the stick can talk. Everyone else must listen until it's their turn to hold the stick.
3. Begin passing the stick around the circle and listening attentively.
4. Let the children say whatever they want, or focus the discussion with a topic or question.
5. The teacher brings closure to the discussion when the stick returns to him or her.

Want to do more?

Pass the talking stick around when telling circle stories. Let children choose to whom they would like to pass the stick. To make a simple talking stick, simply cover a pencil with aluminum foil or wrapping paper. Use the talking stick at the end of the day for children to recall what they have done at school.

★ TRANSITION TIME

Tickets   3+

These tickets make children feel like they're going to do something special and motivate them to be a part of the group.

Words to use

special time
join the group

Materials

colored paper
scissors
can with a plastic
   lid
tape

What to do

1. Using the illustration or your own ideas, make tickets from colored paper.
2. Decorate the can and cut a slit in the lid.
3. As the children arrive in the morning, hand each one a ticket. Tell them to hold on to them so they can come to a special circle time.
4. Encourage the children to put the ticket in their pocket. Tape the tickets to them if they have no pockets, or give the tickets to the children as they clean up.
5. Let the children put their tickets into the slot in the can lid as they join the group.

Want to do more?

Choose a child to help collect the tickets. Make tickets for various centers in the room or for outdoor activities. It might be just what is needed to involve children in new activities.

★ TRANSITION TIME

Table Talk

Enhance language development, social relationships and personal skills with pleasant conversations at lunch and snack.

Words to use

conversation
talk
snack
meal
listening
talking

Materials

What to do

1. When sharing snack or meals with the children, remember that eating together is a meaningful experience as well as a wonderful listening time.
2. Be a good listener.
3. Let the children guide the conversation, or use one of the following suggested topics:
✓ Tell the children about when you were a little girl or boy. Share stories about your personal life, pets, hobbies and family. (You need to be a real person to them!)
✓ Ask them about their birthdays or family vacations.
✓ Talk about how the food tastes. Is it sweet, salty, hard, soft, etc.?
✓ Discuss upcoming events such as a field trip, party, etc.
✓ Ask them about their families, pets, customs and cultures. Emphasize how we are very much alike, but also different.
✓ Relate conversations to a theme, a story or other school activity.
✓ Ask the children about what they like best or least about school.
✓ Engage children in problem-solving a difficulty in the classroom.
✓ Talk about wishes, dreams, nightmares and other feelings.
✓ Listen, listen, listen to what they have to say!

★ TRANSITION TIME

transition activities

Clean-up Time

3

Children learn to clean up their play or learning centers.

Words to use

messy
clean up

Materials

Five Minutes' Peace by Jill Murphy

What to do

1. At the end of free play, the housekeeping corner will invariably look like Mrs. Large's house from *Five Minutes' Peace.*
2. Show the children in the housekeeping corner the picture of Mrs. Large's kitchen, and have them put their housekeeping corner back in order.
3. At circle time, comment on how the children in the housekeeping corner and the dress-up corner found their house looking like Mrs. Large's until they cleaned it up.

Teaching tips

Children enjoy playing, but often balk when asked to clean up. Regularly scheduled clean-up times, five minutes at the end of free play or learning center time, can alleviate the problem. Establish the clean-up time routine by using the same signal each day, a simple song. "It's clean-up time, It's clean-up time, everyone must help, It's clean-up time," or a flick of the light switch, or have a child carry around a clean-up time sign for everyone to see. Most importantly, have a routine and keep the same signal each day until clean-up time goes well. Then, you can change the signal for variety.

★ STORY S-T-R-E-T-C-H-E-R-S

A Different Old MacDonald   3+

Teaches children about farm animals.

Words to use

animals   farm
sounds   eats

Materials

What to do

1. Sing the familiar song "Old MacDonald Had a Farm" as usual, but at the end of each verse, ask the children what the animal named in that verse eats.
2. For example, for the verse that begins "On his farm he had a cow," after the children sing "moo, moo," ask them what a cow eats.
3. Continue singing the song, asking at the end of each verse about the animal named.

★ 500 FIVE MINUTE GAMES

This Little Cow Eats Grass   3+

Teaches children to have fun with rhymes.

Words to use

rhyme   sounds like

Materials

What to do

1. Choose five children to be the cows.
2. Talk about the different things that each cow will do.
3. One cow eats grass—this child pretends to eat grass.
4. Another cow eats hay—this child pretends to eat hay.
5. One cow drinks water—this child pretends to drink water from a pail.
6. Another cow runs away—this child runs across the room.
7. The fifth cow lies down all day—this child lies down on the floor. On the words "chase her, chase her," the fifth child gets up and runs across the room while all the other children chase her.

This little cow eats grass.
This little cow eats hay.
This little cow drinks water.
And this little cow runs away.
This little cow does nothing, but just lies down all day.
We'll chase her, we'll chase her, we'll chase her away.

★ 500 FIVE MINUTE GAMES

Moo, Cow, Moo   3+

Children have to listen very carefully to play this game.

Words to use

circle   middle
blindfold   guess

Materials

blindfold

What to do

1. Seat the children in a circle with one child designated to sit in the middle blindfolded.
2. Everyone sings a favorite song like, "Twinkle, Twinkle, Little Star."
3. The child in the middle can stop the song anytime by saying, "Stop."
4. When she says "Stop," the teacher taps another child on the head, who then says, "Moo, cow, moo."
5. The blindfolded child tries to guess who is making the sounds.
6. Try "bark, dog, bark" or "roar, lion, roar," etc.

★ 500 FIVE MINUTE GAMES

What Would You Do?   3+

Improves children's thinking skills.

Words to use

helpers   job
work

Materials

What to do

1. Talk with the children about different kinds of jobs. Talking about community helpers is often a good way to begin.

2. Recite:

> *What would you do,*
> *What would you do,*
> *What would you do if you*
> *Were a _____ (name a job, for example, police officer)*

3. Choose one child at a time to reply.
4. When that child is finished, ask the others if anyone else has ideas about what he would do if he were a police officer.

★ 500 FIVE MINUTE GAMES

Spider's Web Game   3+

Children practice gross motor skills while playing this Halloween game, a wonderful party activity.

Words to use

yarn
web
string

Materials

black yarn

What to do

1. Set large piece of furniture or gym equipment in the center of your classroom or gym.
2. String the yarn from the equipment to other outlying equipment in the room to form a large spider web covering the game space. Wrap the yarn around table legs, chairs or shelves, and keep returning to the center. Be sure that the strings vary in height.
3. The children, one to three at a time, take turns moving in and out of the spider's web, trying not to get stuck!

★ THE GIANT ENCYCLOPEDIA OF THEME ACTIVITIES

Melt the Witch   3+

Children improve gross motor skills while playing a fun Halloween game.

Words to use

witch
aim
throw

Materials

moveable chalkboard
colored chalk
sponges
bin of water

What to do

1. Draw a witch's head or whole body on the chalkboard (make sure the witch is not too scary looking).
2. Place the board in an area where it will stand alone and not fall over.
3. Fill the bin with water and sponges.
4. The children stand close enough to the board to be able to hit it accurately with a wet sponge. Place water bin and sponges near this spot.
5. Tell children to take turns throwing wet sponges at the witch to try and "melt" her away. (As the witch becomes wet and water drips down the board, it will look like she is melting.) Be sure that children are squeezing out the sponges before throwing!

Want to do more?

Draw other Halloween characters on the board, or let children draw them, and repeat the activity.

★ THE GIANT ENCYCLOPEDIA OF THEME ACTIVITIES

The Farm   4+

Improves children's observation skills.

Words to use

farm   farmer
animal   missing

Materials

What to do

1. Talk about the various animals that live on a farm.
2. Encourage the children to make the sounds of different animals.
3. Choose one child to be the farmer.
4. Tell the rest of the children to pick their favorite farm animal.
5. When you say "go," the children make the sound of that animal.
6. While the children continue to make their sounds, ask the farmer to cover her eyes, because one animal will be going back into the barn.
7. After the farmer's eyes are covered, ask one child to leave the area. Then ask the farmer to guess who is missing.

★ 500 FIVE MINUTE GAMES

Knock, Knock

4+

If you have more than fourteen children, you may have to play the game several times over consecutive days, so everyone will have an opportunity to participate.

Words to use

names
group
class
home
visitor

Materials

two chairs

What to do

1. Arrange the chairs front to back. The front chair is "home," and the back chair is "the visitor."
2. Ask the children to sit together behind the chairs. Ask a volunteer to sit in the home chair and remain facing straight ahead, away from the other children.
3. After the volunteer is seated, point to one of the children, who will quietly take the visitor chair. After being seated, this second child should knock on the home child's chair while saying, "Knock, knock!" The child at home answers, without turning around, "Who's there?" The second child says:

   Listen real well, now you can't see.
   Listen to my voice and then guess me.

4. The child at home names the visitor without turning around. The visitor then goes to the home chair, and another volunteer becomes the visitor.
5. Continue until all the children have been named.

Want to do more?

For added difficulty, have two visitors talking in unison. How about three or four? Can the home child name each visitor?

Book to read

The Perfect Spot by Robert J. Blake

★ THE PEACEFUL CLASSROOM

Rescue Chain

4

Identifying circumstances that are threatening or dangerous is an early step in the development of courage in children. Even though very young children are not capable of real rescues, role playing this aspect of kindness establishes its value.

Words to use

rescue
danger
courage

Materials

chalk or rope, optional

What to do

1. As an introduction to the activity, tell the children the following story.

> *Once upon a time, Penelope Pig decided to go skating on the frozen pond near Butterberry Hill. All of her friends told her, "Don't go skating. The ice is thin, and you might fall in." But Penelope ignored them and went skating anyway. When she was skating in the middle of the pond, the ice broke, and Penelope fell right into the icy water. She was trapped in the ice and sinking fast. When her friends saw her, they wanted to go out on the ice to pull her out. But if they did that then they would fall in, too. They decided to make a rescue chain. Each person held onto the next person's hand as they stretched out to take hold and pull Penelope out. The End.*

2. Ask the children whether they would like to pretend to be like Penelope's friends and rescue her from the icy water. Ask for a volunteer to be Penelope Pig. The rest of the children will make the chain.

3. In a large outdoor space, identify a boundary between the shore and the water. You can draw a line with chalk or stretch out a rope. Place Penelope, sitting on the ground, a sufficient distance from the shore to require a slight stretch in the chain to reach her.

4. Tell the rescuers they have only a few minutes to save Penelope. One rescuer is the anchor, who must remain on shore. You may ask this person to hold onto the branch of a tree or the bar of a jungle gym. The rest of the children make a line, hand in hand, to stretch out to take Penelope's hand. If the line breaks, everyone in the part of the line not connected to the shore will have to sit down to be rescued, too.

5. Ask the children to begin. Cheer them on as they form a line and begin stretching toward Penelope. After a few rounds of the game, talk with the children about the dangers present at a lake or pond at different times of the year.

Want to do more?

To add challenge, decrease the amount of time allowed for the rescue and increase the distance between the shore and Penelope. Of course, do not place Penelope beyond the extreme range of the rescue chain. Another version is to designate two children as the ends of the chain, one the anchor, one the grabber. Play by the same rules as above but blindfold the grabber to simulate a night rescue.

Home connection

While the family watches television, parents can talk with their children about characters who "rescue" others. They can use words like "brave" or "courageous" in their conversations.

★ THE PEACEFUL CLASSROOM

Mystery Person   5+

In this version of "Is It Bigger Than a Bread Box?" children have to depend exclusively on verbal clues for guessing a mystery person's identity. Knowing something about another is an important part of friendship.

Words to use

individual
familiar
guess
clues

Materials

What to do

1. Tell the children that you are thinking about someone in the group and that you would like them to guess who it is. You have some clues to help them guess.
2. Select yourself as the first person to be guessed. Begin with a common characteristic and gradually become more specific. The children raise their hands when they think they know who it is. If, for example, the author began with himself, he might say something like, "This person likes to play with puppets...this person likes fairy tales...this person is a teacher...this person is tall and has a beard...this person is bald."
3. Continue with clues about one of the children in the group.
4. After several rounds of guessing, invite one of the children to select someone and give clues.

Want to do more?

To increase the level of difficulty, give activity clues such as "someone who likes to play in the sand-box," or abstract clues such as "someone who has two brothers and two sisters."

Book to read

Julius, The Baby of the World by Kevin Henkes

Home connection

Parents can try a similar activity at home, including extended family members known to their children as possible "mystery persons."

★ THE PEACEFUL CLASSROOM

Books

Apples and Pumpkins by Anne Rockwell
Around the Year by Elsa Beskow
Barn Dance! by Bill Martin, Jr.
Big Red Barn by Margaret Wise Brown
Chipmunk Song by Joanne Ryder
Early Morning in the Barn by Nancy Tafuri
Farm Morning by David McPhail
The Farmer in the Dell by Kathy Parkinson
From Seed to Pear by Ali Mitgutsch
It Didn't Frighten Me by Janet L. Gross and Jerome C. Harste
It's Halloween by Jack Prelutsky
Johnny Appleseed by Reeve Lindbergh
Leaves by Fulvio Testa
The Little Old Lady Who Was Not Afraid of Anything by Linda Williams
The Magic Pumpkin by Bill Martin, Jr.
My Favorite Time of Year by Susan Pearson
Night in the Country by Cynthia Rylant
Old MacDonald Had a Farm by Carol Jones
Old MacDonald Had a Farm by Glen Rounds
Once There Was a Tree by Natalia Romanova
The Ox Cart Man by Donald Hall
Patchwork Farmer by Craig Brown
The Pumpkin Blanket by Deborah Turney Zagwyn
Pumpkin Pumpkin by Jeanne Titherington
Scary, Scary Halloween by Eve Bunting
The Season's of Arnold's Apple Tree by Gail Gibbons
Squirrels by Brian Wildsmith
The Vanishing Pumpkin by Tony Johnston
The Year at Maple Hill Farm by Alice and Martin Provensen

Records, Tapes and CDs

Beall, Pamela Conn and Susan Hagen Nipp. "Old MacDonald" from *Wee Sing Children's Songs and Fingerplays*. Price Stern Sloan, 1979.

Finkelstein, Mark and Carol. *Everyday's a Holiday*. Melody House. Activity Records, 1971.

Jenkins, Ella. "Did You Feed My Cow?" from *Rosenshontz Tickles You*. RS Records, 1980.

Lucky, Sharron. "The Farmer in the Dell" from *Sing Along with Lucky*. Melody House.

Palmer, Hap. *Witches Brew*. Educational Activities.

Palmer, Hap. *Holiday Songs and Rhythms*. Educational Activities.

Weissman, Jackie. "I Had a Rooster" and "I See a Horse" from *Miss Jackie and Her Friends Sing About Peanut Butter, Tarzan and Roosters*. Miss Jackie, 1981.

"Old MacDonald" from *Sing-A-Long*. Peter Pan, 1989.

NOVEMBER *fall*

Fingerplays, Poems and Songs

Gobble, Gobble, Gobble

Gobble, gobble, gobble
Quack, quack, quack.
A turkey says gobble,
And a duck says quack.

★ ONE POTATO, TWO POTATO, THREE POTATO, FOUR

Peas Porridge Hot

Peas porridge hot, peas porridge cold,
Peas porridge in the pot, nine days old.
Some like it hot, some like it cold.
Some like it in the pot, nine days old.

★ ONE POTATO, TWO POTATO, THREE POTATO, FOUR

Sing a Song of Sixpence

Sing a song of sixpence, a pocket full of rye;
Four and twenty blackbirds baked in a pie.

When the pie was opened, the birds began
   to sing;
Wasn't that a dainty dish to set before the king?

The king was in his counting house counting out
   his money;
The queen was in the parlor eating bread and
   honey.

The maid was in the garden hanging out the
   clothes;
Along came a blackbird and pecked her on her
   nose.

★ ONE POTATO, TWO POTATO, THREE POTATO, FOUR

Over the River and Through the Wood

Over the river and through the wood,
To grandmother's house we go.
The horse knows the way to carry the sleigh
Through the white and drifted snow, oh!
Over the river and through the wood
Oh, how the wind does blow!
It stings the toes and bites the nose,
As over the fields we go!

Over the river and through the wood,
Trot fast, my dapple gray!
Spring over the ground like a hunting hound,
For this is Thanksgiving Day!
Over the river and through the wood,
Now grandmother's cap I spy!
Hurrah for the fun! Is the pudding done?
Hurrah for the pumpkin pie!

Grandma's Spectacles

Here are Grandma's spectacles,
And here is Grandma's hat;
And here's the way she folds her hands
And puts them in her lap.

Oh Where, Oh Where Has My Little Dog Gone?

Oh where, oh where has my little dog gone?
Oh where, oh where can he be?
With his ears cut short and his tail cut long,
Oh where, oh where can he be?

★ WHERE IS THUMBKIN?

She'll Be Comin' 'Round the Mountain

She'll be comin' 'round the mountain when she
    comes,
She'll be comin' 'round the mountain when she
    comes,
She'll be comin' 'round the mountain,
She'll be comin' 'round the mountain,
She'll be comin' 'round the mountain when she
    comes.

She'll be driving six white horses when she comes,
She'll be driving six white horses when she comes,
She'll be driving six white horses,
She'll be driving six white horses,
She'll be driving six white horses when she
    comes.

We'll all have chicken and dumplin's when she
    comes,
We'll all have chicken and dumplin's when she
    comes,
We'll all have chicken and dumplin's,
We'll all have chicken and dumplin's,
We'll all have chicken and dumplin's when she
    comes.

★ WHERE IS THUMBKIN?

Five Fat Turkeys Are We

Five fat turkeys are we.
We slept all night in a tree.
When the cook came
    around,
We couldn't be found
    and,
That's why we're here you
    see!

Oh, five fat turkeys are
    we.
We spent all night in a tree.
It sure does pay on Thanksgiving day,
To sleep in the tallest tree.

★ WHERE IS THUMBKIN?

Go Tell Aunt Rhody

Go tell Aunt Rhody,
Go tell Aunt Rhody,
Go tell Aunt Rhody,
Her old gray goose is dead.

The one we've been saving,
The one we've been saving,
The one we've been saving,
To make a feather bed.

She died on Friday,
She died on Friday,
She died on Friday,
With an aching in her head.

Old gander's weeping,
Old gander's weeping
Old gander's weeping
Because his wife's dead.

Goslings are mourning,
Goslings are mourning,
Goslings are mourning,
Because their mother's dead.

Go tell Aunt Rhody,
Go tell Aunt Rhody,
Go tell Aunt Rhody,
Her old gray goose is dead.

★ WHERE IS THUMBKIN?

The More We Get Together

Tune: "Did You Ever See a Lassie?"
The more we get together,
Together, together,
The more we get together,
The happier are we.

For your friends are my friends,
And my friends are your friends,
The more we get together,
The happier are we.

★ WHERE IS THUMBKIN?

November Learning Centers

Music and Sound Center

While playing in the Music and Sound Center children learn:

1. To enjoy making music and participating in musical activities.
2. To explore sounds produced by many different objects and instruments.
3. To listen to a variety of music.
4. To enhance their self-concept as they learn new ways of expressing their feelings.

Suggested Props for the Music and Sound Center

rhythm instruments including
- ✓ rhythm sticks
- ✓ sand blocks
- ✓ drums
- ✓ triangles
- ✓ cymbals
- ✓ xylophone
- ✓ bells
- ✓ shakers

cassette tape player and tapes (include a variety of performers on recordings: children singing, professional performers, orchestras and bands)

tapes of music from different cultures with appropriate instruments

tapes of different types of music (folk, classical, bluegrass, rap or rock)

During the early years, it is important to expose children to a variety of music as they begin to develop preferences.

Curriculum Connections

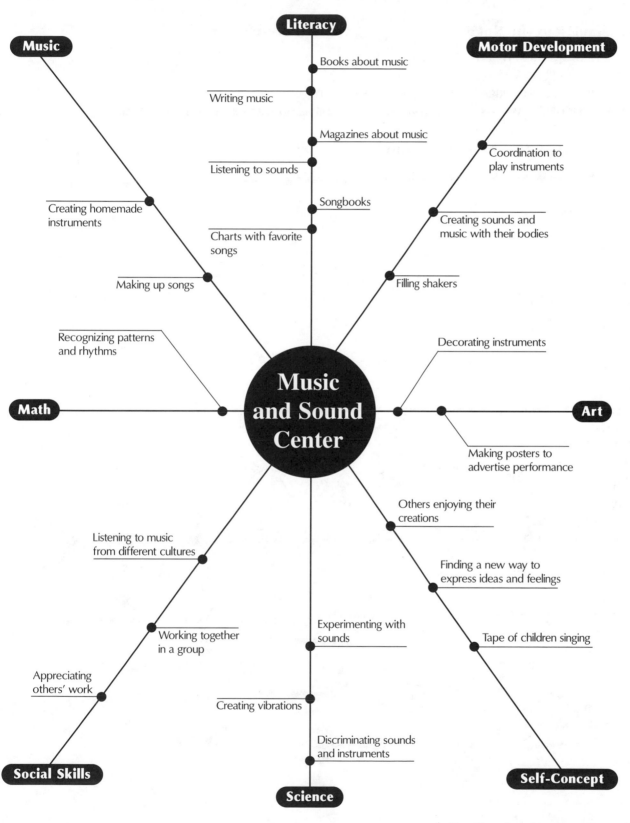

Literacy
- Books about music
- Writing music
- Magazines about music
- Listening to sounds
- Songbooks
- Charts with favorite songs

Music
- Creating homemade instruments
- Making up songs
- Recognizing patterns and rhythms

Motor Development
- Coordination to play instruments
- Creating sounds and music with their bodies
- Filling shakers

Math

Art
- Decorating instruments
- Making posters to advertise performance

Social Skills
- Listening to music from different cultures
- Working together in a group
- Appreciating others' work

Self-Concept
- Others enjoying their creations
- Finding a new way to express ideas and feelings
- Tape of children singing

Science
- Experimenting with sounds
- Creating vibrations
- Discriminating sounds and instruments

Music and Sound Center

★ THE COMPLETE LEARNING CENTER BOOK

Bakery/Cooking Center

While playing in the Bakery/Cooking Center children learn:

1. To work cooperatively to make a product.
2. To use reading and writing in functional ways.
3. To develop their language while they discuss cooking experiences.
4. To learn about the work of people in the community and the services they provide.

Suggested Props for the Bakery/Cooking Center

cash register
cooking utensils such as
   measuring tools
   rolling pins
   cookie sheets
   pie pans
   large bowl
   hand turned mixer
   large spoons, etc.

Curriculum Connections

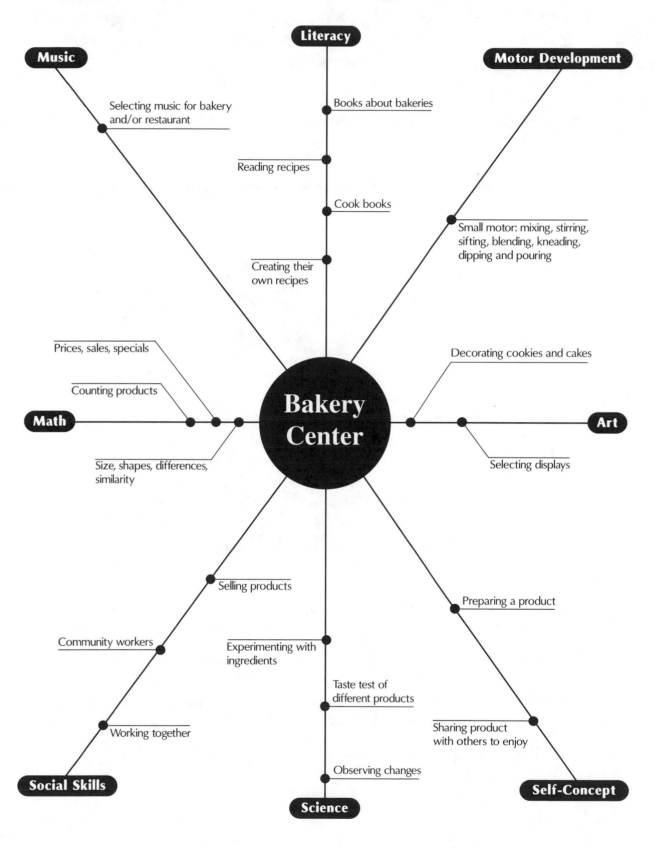

Music

Selecting music for bakery and/or restaurant

Literacy

Books about bakeries

Reading recipes

Cook books

Creating their own recipes

Motor Development

Small motor: mixing, stirring, sifting, blending, kneading, dipping and pouring

Math

Prices, sales, specials

Counting products

Size, shapes, differences, similarity

Bakery Center

Decorating cookies and cakes

Art

Selecting displays

Selling products

Community workers

Working together

Social Skills

Experimenting with ingredients

Taste test of different products

Observing changes

Science

Preparing a product

Sharing product with others to enjoy

Self-Concept

NOVEMBER

Art Activities

Nature's People

3+

These little characters take on their own personalities depending on the materials used and the clothes added.

Words to use

nuts
head
body
clothes

Materials

assorted nuts in the shell—filberts (also called hazelnuts), acorns, walnuts, etc.
pine cones, nut casings, acorn caps, etc.—whatever is available in your area
tacky glue is good because it is fast drying—or use white glue or carpenter's glue
bits of wool felt for clothing
scissors
black felt pen

What to do

1. Select two nuts, pine cones or other natural material and glue one on top of the other to make a head and body. Position them according to the "character" you wish to create. For example, filberts have pointy ends that make a nice face. Some nuts have flat tops that are good places to attach heads. Acorn "tops" make good caps. Some pine cones have flat bottoms; these make good bodies.
2. Add a scarf, hat, shirt, cloak and any other clothing by gluing on bits of felt.
3. Use a felt pen to add dots for eyes, but do not draw in all the features. Leave that to the children's imagination.
4. Play with these little people in the sand box or in little towns or scenes the children create. They are delightful peeking out of a table's centerpiece.

★ EARTHWAYS

Fall Lanterns

As the days grow shorter, we all need to prepare for the cold days and long nights. The lantern is a symbol of this. Send the lantern home to be used as a lovely autumn centerpiece or the focus of a special nighttime lantern walk.

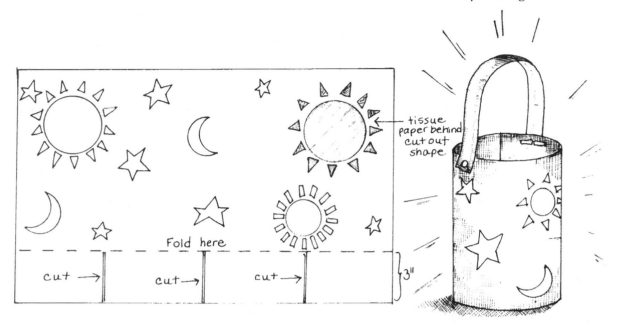

Words to use

lantern
light
dark
shine

Materials

heavy construction paper or heavy white watercolor paper approximately 9" x 12" or 12" x 16".
   Size is not crucial, so you can experiment a bit.
crayons or liquid watercolors and paintbrushes
scissors
stapler
tacky glue, white or glue sticks
paper fasteners or 1/4 inch wire (florists' wire)
warming candles, votive candles or tea lights (available at grocery, hardware or kitchen stores)
masking tape
tissue paper, optional

What to do

1. The children decorate their lantern papers by coloring or painting them. Suns, moons and stars are appropriate decorations, but the younger children will just make color designs. Let the children choose how to color or paint their lanterns. Encourage them to fill the paper with color.

2. Make a fold all the way across the length of the paper, approximately three inches up from the bottom.

3. Cut a fringe of three-inch wide segments all along the bottom folded section.

4. Cut several small shapes out of the top portion of the lantern. These are the "windows" that the light shines through; they can be circles, random shapes or shapes cut in the sun, stars and moon motif. The sun can be just a circular cutout with snips or colored "rays." Older children can cut their own shapes though they may need help starting the cuts. Small pieces of colored tissue paper glued over the inside of windows create a beautiful effect.

5. Form the lantern paper into a cylinder, stapling it at the top and bottom. Fold the fringed edges in and overlap them to make the lantern's bottom. Put small dabs of glue between the fringes to hold them together.

6. Add a fairly long handle (12-15 inches) of either 1/4 inch wire poked through the sides and twisted back up onto itself to secure it or cut 1/2-inch wide strips and attach them to each side of the lantern with paper fasteners.

7. For the light use votive candles, warming candles or tea lights that come in individual metal cups. A loop of masking tape placed in the bottom of the lantern holds the candle in place.

Note: As with all activities involving candles, children should never use their lanterns unsupervised. Also, never leave lanterns burning when you are not nearby.

★ EARTHWAYS

Family Pictures

3+

Helps children learn creative expression while developing fine motor skills.

Words to use

family
names
pictures

Materials

drawing paper
crayons

What to do

1. Ask the children to draw pictures of their families.
2. Label the people in each drawing and display the pictures on the bulletin board.

★ WHERE IS THUMBKIN?

NOVEMBER

art activities

194

My House, Your House

3+

Children learn to compare their homes with their friends' homes.

Words to use

house   home
apartment   windows
doors

Materials

drawing paper
crayons or markers

What to do

1. Have the children draw "house" pictures. Younger preschoolers will recall features of their houses and their friends' without trying to separate likenesses and differences.
2. After the children have completed their pictures, ask if it is their house or one of their friends' houses. Note their responses on their papers.
3. Older preschoolers can make two drawings, one for the things that are the same and one for the things that are different.

Teaching tips

If your children have had little experience visiting friends' homes, then encourage comparisons of "My Home" and "My School."

★ STORY S-T-R-E-T-C-H-E-R-S

Weather Pictures

3+

Children learn to draw what is happening because of the weather.

Words to use

weather   draw
wind   snow
rain   sun
clouds

Materials

Out and About by Shirley Hughes
paper
crayons or markers

What to do

1. Look through all of Shirley Hughes' double page illustrations of the weather.
2. Discuss what the weather is like today and what people are doing because of the weather.
3. Ask the children to draw weather pictures.
4. Display the pictures on a weather bulletin board.

Teaching tips

Onto a sheet of construction paper, print one of Shirley Hughes' poems that describes the present weather. Center it in your display of the children's weather drawings.

★ STORY S-T-R-E-T-C-H-E-R-S

Fuzzy Glue Drawing   3+

Sometimes pictures are made with yarn.

Words to use

yarn
glue

Materials

scissors
yarn in contrasting colors to the background
plastic bag or plastic container with lid for yarn snips
white glue in a dish (to color white glue, mix with food coloring or tempera paint)
paintbrush for glue
paper plate or matte board for the base
covered work surface

What to do

1. Wind some yarn around your fingers about fifteen times—but not too tight. Cut through the end of the loops.
2. Snip small pieces of the yarn one-half inch or smaller into the plastic bag or container. (Cut different lengths or different colors if desired.)
3. Paint glue over a small area of the base.
4. Choose a color of yarn and pat it down into the glued area.
5. Paint more glue in a different area and pat more yarn into that glue. Continue making glue and yarn designs or continue until the entire base is full.

Want to do more?

Cut different colors of yarn and draw a picture with a glue bottle to create fuzzy yarn pictures. Always work on small areas rather than large areas so glue won't dry out before the yarn has been attached.

Teaching tips

The one trick to a successful project is to spread the glue onto the base and press the yarn into the glue. Do not dip the yarn into the glue in the dish. Adults can help with hand-wiping and yarn-snipping but the artists should draw and cover the glue pictures.

★ PRESCHOOL ART

Stringing Necklaces   4+

These easy-to-make necklaces are autumn treasures.

Words to use

kernels
swell
needle
thread
necklace

Materials

Indian corn kernels
large bowl
water
long strands of heavy thread
    (button-hose twist or
    embroidery floss)
heavy sewing needles
masking tape and pen
towel

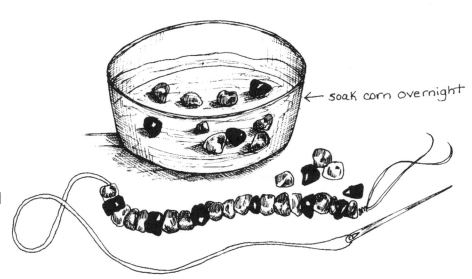

← soak corn overnight

What to do

1. Soak a large quantity of the corn kernels in a bowl of water overnight. It's fun for the children to help you set this up the day before you plan to string the necklaces. If you plan to grind the corn, save several cups of kernels for that—they will grind more easily if they haven't been soaked first.
2. In the morning, pour off the water and bring the bowl of corn to the work table. The children love to dip their hands in and "finger" the damp corn that has softened and swelled a bit overnight.
3. Give each child who is ready to work a needle threaded with 24 inches of doubled thread. Tie a knot about two inches from the end. Using doubled thread will keep the thread from slipping off the needles.
Note: Be sure to show the children how to use a needle properly. Supervise closely.
4. The children choose the kernels they want, push the needle through the center of each kernel (be careful of little fingers here) and slide the kernel down to the knot. It's helpful to start with the kernel resting on the table, rather than holding it, and just push the needle down through the kernel.

5. The children thread as many (or as few) kernels as they want, again leaving about two inches of thread at the other end. To continue this activity over a few days, just mark each string with the child's name (masking tape works well) and keep the unused corn kernels moist by covering them with a damp towel and refrigerating them so they don't get moldy.

6. When the necklaces are finished, center the corn kernels if they aren't a full string and tie the open ends together in a bow around the children's necks.

7. Some of the corn may begin to sprout—a perfect opportunity to grow some corn planted indoors to be transplanted to your garden in the spring. Then you can harvest your own Indian corn next fall.

★ EARTHWAYS

String Thing

4+

Make a string balloon!

Words to use

balloon
string

Materials

granulated starch
water
pan
stove
spoon
bowl
colorful yarn or embroidery floss, about 1 yard long
a strong balloon
table covered with newspaper

What to do

1. With adult help, make this extra strong liquid starch: dissolve one tablespoon of granulated starch in the amount of water stated on the starch package. Follow the rest of the instructions on the package. Place in a bowl and cool.
2. Blow up a balloon. Tie a double knot at the end.
3. Dip a string or yarn in the starch mixture. Make sure it is completely covered with starch but not too heavy to drape around the balloon.
4. Wrap the string around the balloon being sure to plaster down the ends of the string.
5. When the balloon is well covered with string (but not completely covered), dry the balloon overnight.
6. When the string is thoroughly dry, pop the balloon and remove it.
7. Use a piece of thread to hang the String Thing from the ceiling, a branch or from some other framework.

Teaching tips

The tendency to over-wrap the balloon is common. If too much string is used, it will just slip off the balloon in a pile on the table. Begin again and use less string. Gently squeeze some of the starch out of the yarn between two fingers and the yarn will be sticky but not too heavy.

★ Preschool Art

Cuff Finger Puppets   4+

Recycle an old pair of pants into these creative finger puppets.

Words to use

puppet
finger
story

Materials

old pair of pants with deep cuffs or
    hem
sewing machine
scissors
materials for decorating the puppets
    including sewing scraps, yarn, but-
    tons, plastic eyes or felt
tacky glue or needle and thread

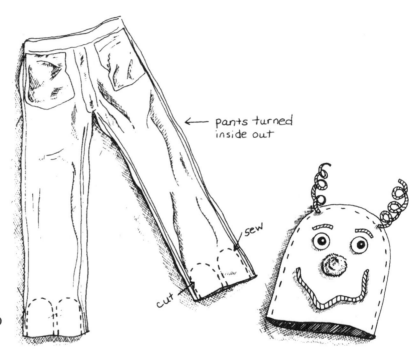

← pants turned inside out

sew

cut

What to do

1. Turn an old pair of pants with deep cuffs inside out. Cut straight across the hem.
2. With adult help sew two "U" shapes on each cuff so that the hem of the cuff will be the bottom of each finger puppet. Cut one-third inch from the edge of the sewn line. Turn the cuff right-side out or leave as is.
3. Decorate the cuff puppets with any variety of sewing or craft items using glue or a needle and thread. Puppets can be animals, people, characters from a book or story or strange little shapes with no real adult understanding.
4. Make up plays, songs or simply enjoy the puppets.

Want to do more?

Decorate a box for storing a growing collection of cuff puppets. Develop a group of puppets that can be stored together such as the three cuff bears and one golden-haired cuff girl.

★ Preschool Art

Easy Store Puppet Stage

4+

Create an easy-to-make and easy-to-store puppet stage.

Words to use

sheet
doorway
curtain
stage

Materials

one spring-tension curtain
    rod to fit a doorway
old sheet cut to fit the
    doorway opening
fabric pen
glue paints (tacky glue and
    tempera paint mixed
    together)
dishes for paints
paintbrushes
sewing machines, optional

What to do

1. Spread a spring-tension
   curtain rod in a doorway
   at a height suitable for
   young puppeteers.
2. With fabric pens or glue paint, decorate an old sheet for the puppet curtain. Dry the curtain completely.
3. Drape the sheet over the rod and produce a puppet show by crouching behind the curtain.
4. As an optional idea, sew a simple casing at the top of a decorated sheet cut to fit the doorway and rod. Push the curtain rod through the casing and place it in the doorway.
5. To store the puppet stage, roll the curtain up around the rod and put it in any corner or spare closet space.

Want to do more?

Make a glamorous curtain by adding glitter, hobby jewels or beads to the wet glue paint.

Teaching tips

Remember that sometimes puppeteers need help winding up a long production with a gentle hint that the show will end in a few more minutes.

★ PRESCHOOL ART

Thanksgiving Handy Turkey

4+

Children will have fun with this Thanksgiving activity, while improving their fine motor skills.

Words to use

turkey
feathers
wattle
beak

Materials

6" x 9" construction paper, different colors
markers
scissors
glue or stapler

What to do

1. Trace shoe on brown paper and cut out to make the turkey's body.
2. Trace hand with fingers spread apart on other colors of construction paper and cut out to make feathers.
3. Glue or staple feathers onto turkey's body.
4. Draw or make a wattle, eyes and beak from the leftover scrap paper.

Want to do more?

Staple the turkey to a lunch bag to make a puppet.

★ The Giant Encyclopedia of Theme Activities

Wheat Weaving

5+

*Braided wheat straw decorations are symbols of good luck and prosperity.
They are part of harvest celebrations in many lands.*

Words to use

braid
wheat
harvest

Materials

wheat on the stalk—from craft supply stores or from farmers in your area who grow wheat
tub of water
red yarn or embroidery floss

What to do

1. Names of farmers in your area who grow wheat are often available from the local county extension service or 4-H clubs.
2. Soak the wheat stems (be sure the seed heads are out of the water) in the tub of water for about an hour before you want to use them.
3. The children work in pairs with one holding the seed heads and the other one braiding. Give one child in each pair three stalks of wheat. Help the children start braiding the stems, beginning at the end near the seed heads.
4. Do a simple braid. Chanting the following helps.
   Put the right one in the middle.
   Put the left one in the middle.
   Repeat the chant as needed.
5. Make the braid fairly tight, and braid the entire stem.
6. Curve the braided end around, overlapping it with the seed heads and tie with a yarn bow.
7. These make lovely additions to the Season's Garden or decorations for the snack table, especially at a harvest celebration. They also make great napkin holders!

Want to do more?

Play a weaving ring game with the children. Stand in a circle, holding hands, and chant or sing (just make up a simple tune) the following:

> *Harvest crown, harvest crown*
> *Now we weave a harvest crown.*
> *(Susie) weaves and (Nathan) weaves*
> *Now we weave a harvest crown.*

Name two children standing side by side. When the children are named, they cross their arms in front of them and re-make the circle, holding hands with crossed arms. Gradually sing your way around the circle, calling pairs of children to weave until you've "woven" the whole circle (all the children have crossed their arms and are holding the hands of the children next to them). After the last pair, sing or chant:

> *Harvest crown, harvest crown*
> *Now we've woven our harvest crown.*

This is a very simple little game, but the children never cease to wonder at the weaving of it. The little ones may need help crossing their arms, and be sure to stand close enough together in the circle so that the children can reach each other.

★ EARTHWAYS

Feeling Face Masks   5+

Feelings are often confused with behavior. We treat some emotions with disdain because of the association we make between feelings and behavior—anger with hitting, fear with running away, for example. But emotions are not "bad." Actions may be harmful and beliefs irrational, but emotions are a natural part of being human. As you respond to children's behavior, make statements like, "I know you feel angry, but I cannot allow you to hit Cindy. No hitting in our school."

Words to use

happy
sad
angry
afraid

Materials

one large paper bag for each child
four bags upon which are drawn either a happy, angry, sad or frightened face
mask materials (crayons, construction paper, yarn, paste or glue, etc.)
scissors
large mirror

What to do

1. Show all the materials to the children when they arrive at the art area. Suggest that they try to make masks with happy, angry, sad or frightened faces. Help them make holes at eye level so that they can place the bags over their heads and see what they look like.
2. Put out the paper bags and materials and encourage the children to draw their own "feeling faces." While the masks are being made, discuss various feelings, how they originate and their consequences.
3. Display the masks you made earlier if the children need help understanding what to do. Do not, however, use your masks as models for children to copy. Let them create their own.
4. When the children have finished, invite them to guess what kinds of feelings the others have drawn on their masks.
5. Under close supervision, invite the children to wear the masks and see what they look like in the mirror.

Note: Never allow a child to wear such a mask unattended.

Want to do more?

Masks can also be made from large paper plates using a rubber band stapled to the side as a headband.

★ THE PEACEFUL CLASSROOM

Circle Time and Group Activities

Gilberto and the Wind

3+

Teaches children about the wind.

Words to use

blow
whisper
howl

Materials

Gilberto and the Wind by Marie Hall Ets

What to do

1. Ask the children to look outside the classroom window and decide if the wind is blowing. What do they see that lets them know the wind is blowing? Is it brisk or calm? Would it sound like a whisper in our ears or a howl?
2. Show the children the cover of *Gilberto and the Wind* and ask whether or not they think the wind is blowing.
3. Read the book through once without pausing to discuss Gilberto's fun with the wind.
4. Read it a second time and pause several times in the book for children to talk about similar experiences.

★ MORE STORY S-T-R-E-T-C-H-E-R-S

The Tiny Seed

3+

Teaches about the life cycle of a seed.

Words to use

seed
wind
grow

Materials

The Tiny Seed by Eric Carle
a sunflower seed for each child

What to do

1. Place a sunflower seed in each child's hand to hold while you read the story.
2. Ask the children to imagine that this tiny seed is being blown by the wind.
3. Read *The Tiny Seed* and pause to ask the children what will happen to the little seed when the big foot is about to step on it and when the petals are being blown away.

★ STORY S-T-R-E-T-C-H-E-R-S

Family Hats   3+

Teaches children about the roles and responsibilities of family members.

Words to use

family
father
mother
sister
brother

Materials

variety of hats

What to do

1. Pile the hats in the middle of the circle. Teach the children the following song to the tune of "Pop Goes the Weasel."

> *Marching around the family hats*
> *So early in the morning.*
> *I'll pick one up and put it on*
> *Now I'm my (family member).*

2. Ask one child to march around the pile of hats while the group sings the song. The child picks out one hat, puts it on and says which member of his family might wear a hat like that.
3. The child says something about the family member he has chosen or the child pretends to be that family member.
4. The child puts the hat back in the middle of the circle. Continue until everyone has had a turn. Make sure you take a turn yourself.
5. Say this poem:

> *These are Grandfather's glasses (circle fingers around eyes)*
> *And this is Grandfather's hat (place hands on head)*
> *And this is the way he folds his arms (fold arms across chest)*
> *Just like that!*
> *These are Grandmother's glasses....*

Want to do more?

Art: Make paper plate portraits using 9" round plates. Provide a variety of yarn, fabric scraps, wiggly eyes and other materials. Display the creations on a bulletin board titled "Our Families."

Dramatic play: Add the collection of hats to the dramatic play area. Encourage the children to use the props to role play the people in their families.

Language: Ask the children to draw and color a portrait of the family member they chose to role play. Write what the child says about the person on the drawing and bind all of the pictures together into a class book.

Books to read

Away Went the Farmer's Hat by Jane B. Moncure
Grandpa's Great City Tour by James Stevenson
Hats, Hats, Hats by Ann Morris
Lyle Finds His Mother by Bernard Waber
Mufaro's Beautiful Daughters by John Steptoe
Song and Dance Man by Karen Ackerman
The Napping House by Don and Audrey Wood
Uncle Elephant by Arnold Lobel

★ THE GIANT ENCYCLOPEDIA OF CIRCLE TIME AND GROUP ACTIVITIES

Yesterday, Today and Tomorrow   3+

Use this activity to review what children did yesterday and to plan for the new day.

Words to use

yesterday
today
tomorrow
calendar
plan

Materials

3 large envelopes
12" x 24" poster board
glue
markers
7 index cards, 4" x 6"

What to do

1. Cut off the tops of the envelopes, then glue them to the poster board to make pockets. Write yesterday, today and tomorrow on the envelopes.

2. Print a day of the week on the top of each index card.
3. After referring to the classroom calendar and talking about the date, place the appropriate cards in the envelopes saying, "Yesterday was (name day of week). Today is (name day of week). Tomorrow will be (name day of week)."
4. Ask the children to share what they did in school yesterday, then ask them to say what they plan to do today.
5. Build anticipation and interest by planning something special for tomorrow.

Want to do more?

Use this activity at the end of the day to help children recall what they learned and to build excitement for the coming day. Choose a child to be the calendar helper. This child places the appropriate cards in the envelopes.

★ TRANSITION TIME

Emotions Picture File

3+

Some children have no words to express how they feel. They need to hear such words as "happy," "sad," "angry," and "afraid" if they are to understand their emotional experiences. With younger children, begin with basic emotions and progress to complex emotions which are more difficult to understand.

Words to use

Basic emotions

anger	sadness
fear/afraid	happy

Complex emotions

excitement	disgust
jealousy	courage
boredom	love

Materials

a collection of pictures cut from magazines, each showing children or adults experiencing one of the emotions listed above—glue pictures to identical sizes of heavy construction paper or card stock and number pictures on the back and laminate

What to do

1. Activity 1: During circle time, hold up one of the pictures and ask the children how this person feels. (If they do not know, tell them.) Ask the children to talk about what they see that makes them think the person feels that way. Point out facial expressions or other features which suggest the emotion.
2. Activity 2: Stack at least three pictures of each emotion on a table in your classroom. Mix up the order of the pictures. Hand the stack to a child and ask him to group all the sad pictures together, then all the happy ones and so on.

3. Activity 3: Either at a table or during circle time, show several pictures portraying the same emotion and ask the children to identify how all the people feel.

Home connection

Urge parents to use simple words like "angry," "happy," "sad" and "frightened" as they talk with their children.

★ THE PEACEFUL CLASSROOM

Poor Little Sad Eyes   3+

Criticizing how children express their feelings will not make those feelings disappear. Telling a child what not to do is inadequate. If we do not like a child's behavior, we have to show her what to do to manage her emotions.

Words to use

sad   cry
tears   emotions

Materials

What to do

1. At circle time, read and act out the following poem:

> *Poor little boy with sad eyes, (point to eyes)*
> *See him now, how much he cries, (mimic crying, hands to eyes)*
> *He tries to stop with all his might, (clench teeth, grimace)*
> *He doesn't know (shake head)*
> *That tears are all right. (nod head "yes" while pointing to "tears")*

2. Repeat the poem with the children joining in both the words and actions.
3. Ask the children if they think it is okay for boys and daddies to cry. How about girls and mommies? Invite them to talk about a time when they were sad.

Want to do more?

Make up your own poems about anger, fear and happiness, emphasizing behavior that is acceptable.

Book to read

Christmas Moon by Denys Cazet

Home connection

If you have the opportunity to meet with the parents as a group, explore with them acceptable ways to express emotion, especially anger. Send home the poem for parents to read with their children. Encourage them to talk with their children about a time they cried.

★ THE PEACEFUL CLASSROOM

Sorting Gourds

4+

A wide assortment of gourds in all different shapes and sizes increases the fun and learning in this activity.

Words to use

gourd
color
texture
size

Materials

assortment of gourds in a basket
(at least 1 gourd per child)
large grid and name tags for
graphing, optional

What to do

1. At circle time, show and talk about gourds that people use as decorations in their homes in the fall.
2. Look at the gourds and ask the children to say in what ways the gourds are similar and in what ways they are different (consider size, color, texture).
3. Let each child select one gourd from the basket. Ask each child to tell something about her gourd.
4. Ask the children to get in groups according to one characteristic of the gourds (consider size, color, texture). Designate areas around the circle where each group should line up.
5. Count the number of children in each line. Which group is largest? Which is the smallest?

Want to do more?

Science: Ask the children to predict what will be inside each gourd, then cut them open to find out. Are there seeds? What are seeds for? What do the seeds look like? How many seeds are there? What else is inside?

Book to read

Pumpkin, Pumpkin by Jeanne Titherington

★ THE GIANT ENCYCLOPEDIA OF CIRCLE TIME AND GROUP ACTIVITIES

ood for the Hungry

4+

Young children who have never known prolonged hunger cannot comprehend the experience of those who have. Young children can, however, understand that they are doing something to help others by bringing the food to school.

Words to use

hunger
nutrition
generosity

Materials

paper
several cans of vegetables, soup or fruit to serve as extras

What to do

1. Contact your local food bank to make arrangements for bringing in food donations.
2. Write a brief letter to the parents of your children describing your food drive. Tell them the date you would like to have the children bring one can of food to the school for a local food bank.
3. During circle time, discuss briefly the problem that some children and their families in your community have with hunger. Tell them you will send a letter home to their parents asking them to donate a can of food for their children to give to the hungry.
4. Discuss why good, nutritious food is important and suggest different types of foods that are needed.
5. On the day of the food drive, give a can of food to the children who did not bring one from home. When all the children have arrived, ask them to bring their cans of food to circle time. Go around the circle, each child identifying the food she brought. Thank each child individually. Briefly describe how a hungry person would react to the food they brought. You might say, "Oh, those peaches will taste so good. Peaches will help make a hungry person healthy."
6. Try to arrange for your class to bring the food to the food bank. If this is not possible, perhaps someone from the food bank would visit your class to pick up the food and talk with the children.

Want to do more?

Instead of food, the children can bring in an old toy for distribution to needy children during the winter holidays.

Book to read

Winter Harvest by Jane Chelsea Aragon

Home connection

Parents can involve their children in deciding which food to provide. What food would be the best to choose? A can of peaches is better and more nutritious than a bag of marshmallows.

★ THE PEACEFUL CLASSROOM

NOVEMBER

circle time activities

My Family Tree   5+

Teaches about how families love and help each other.

Words to use

families   help
responsible   family tree

Materials

crayons   scissors
glue   markers
Love You Forever by Robert Munsch
large sheets of white construction paper
sheets of construction paper (various colors)

What to do

1. At circle time talk about families. What things do we do with our families? How do we help each other? What responsibilities do we each have?
2. Read *Love You Forever* and talk about the story.
3. Take the children outside to look for leaves. Ask each child to gather four or five leaves.
4. Let children choose different colors of construction paper to trace their leaves onto (one leaf per family member). Cut out the shapes of the leaves.
5. Distribute large sheets of white construction paper. Ask the children to draw a large tree and at the top or bottom of the sheet write "My Family Tree." Down the trunk of the tree ask the children to write their family's last name. (The teacher may help the children write, if needed.)
6. Then, the children write (or teacher writes) the names of their family members on the leaves they have cut out. Glue the leaves onto the tree to make a family tree.

Want to do more?

Math: Graph the number of family members each child has. Which family has the most family members? Which family has the least? Then, individually, ask each child to graph the number of family members in their own family who have a certain specified characteristic (color of hair or eyes).

Science: Choose one recipe from family favorites to prepare with the class. Involve the children measuring the ingredients. Notice the differences in the food before and after baking or freezing. Taste the food after it has been prepared. How does it taste? Salty? Sweet? Bitter?

Writing: As a class, construct a cookbook. Ask each child to think of his favorite family recipe (it can be anything they like to eat). Ask each child to write his version of the recipe, the ingredients and measurements that he thinks are in the recipe. Combine all the recipes into a cookbook. Duplicate copies so that each child has one to give as a gift to family members. Keep the original copy of the cookbook to be added to the reading center.

Books to read

All Kinds of Families by Norma Simon
I Go with My Family to Grandma's by Rikki Levinson
Nana Upstairs, Nana Downstairs by Tomie dePaola
The Terrible Thing That Happened at Our House by Marge Blaine

Dramatic Play Activities

Show This Feeling with Your Face   3+

Children imitate or improvise facial expressions to show a variety of emotions.

Words to use

face
express

Materials

mirror, optional

What to do

1. Each child picks a partner. They watch each other's faces.
2. Name some emotions at random. The children try to show each other these feelings. Expect a lot of giggles.
3. Mention a range of emotions, including a sense of accomplishment (pride), happiness, anger, feeling secure, being frustrated, feeling surprised.

Teaching tips

Young children will be able to make the facial expression better if they have mirrors. Older children might enjoy making expression and letting their partners try to figure out what emotion they are expressing. If the partner has difficulty guessing, then as additional clues, let the "expressor" tell a situation where this emotion might happen.

★ MORE STORY S-T-R-E-T-C-H-E-R-S

A Home for Puppy   3+

What fun it is to pretend to be a puppy!

Words to use

puppy
dog
house

Materials

large cardboard box (washing machine or dryer box would be great)
scissors or box cutter
tempera paint
paintbrushes

What to do

1. Cut a door in one side of the box.
2. With the children's help, paint and decorate the box to create a dog house.
3. Use the home for dramatic play.

★ WHERE IS THUMBKIN?

Chef Hats

3+

These props will help children feel like "real" chefs.

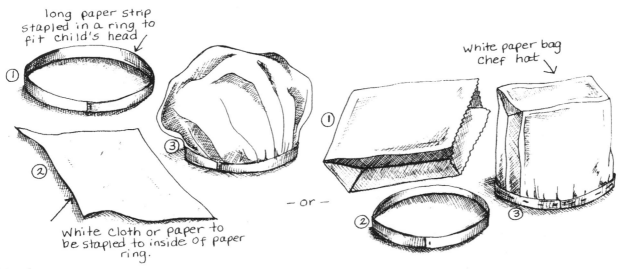

① long paper strip stapled in a ring to fit child's head

②

③

White cloth or paper to be stapled to inside of paper ring.

— or —

① white paper bag chef hat

②

③

Words to use

chef   cook
bake   food

Materials

poster board   old sheets or white paper bags
scissors   stapler

What to do

1. Construct chef hats out of old sheets or white paper bags and poster board.
2. Staple the top piece to a head band made of poster board.
3. The children, with adult help, write their names or the name of the bakery on their hats.
4. Make simple aprons out of sheets and decorate with markers or trim them with material glued to the fabric.

★ THE COMPLETE LEARNING CENTER BOOK

Shakers

3+

Develops fine motor skills and a sense of tone.

Words to use

shaker   sound
high   low

Materials

aluminum cans
beans, rice, bells, nuts, pennies, nails, rocks
masking tape or contact paper

What to do

1. Create shakers that vary in the sound they produce.
2. Fill aluminum cans with beans, rice, bells, nuts, pennies, nails or rocks.
3. Let the children select the material and the quantity they want to place inside the can.
4. Cover the opening with masking tape or a piece of contact paper.
5. Decorate the outside of the can with small pieces of contact paper.
6. Each shaker will produce a different sound.
7. The children use the shakers to make music or accompany their singing in the Music and Sound Center or any time they sing or dance.

★ THE COMPLETE LEARNING CENTER BOOK

Pantomime Stories

4+

Teaches children how to retell a story using only motions.

Words to use

actions
pantomime
story

Materials

books or stories such as *The Snowy Day* by Ezra Jack Keats, optional

What to do

1. Read a story, such as *The Snowy Day* by Ezra Jack Keats.
2. Let one or several children pantomime the activity of the lead character as he looks for the snowball in his pocket, makes angels in the snow, etc.
3. Tell the story again and let another child, or a few children, interpret the story as he visualizes the actions.

★ THE INSTANT CURRICULUM

Language Activities

Silly Sentences

3+

A silly, fun way to learn about rhyming.

Words to use

rhyme
silly
sentence

Materials

What to do

1. Create a series of rhyming silly sentences for children to repeat. For example:

> *I know a lady with knobby knees.*
> *Who's always eating cheddar cheese.*
>
> *I like ice cream in my soup.*
> *By myself or in a group.*

★ THE INSTANT CURRICULUM

Rhyme Time

3+

Children learn that rhyming helps them remember what comes next.

Words to use

rhyme   nursery rhyme
What comes next?

Materials

nursery rhyme book

What to do

1. Read familiar nursery rhymes.
2. Stop at the end rhyming word and let the children supply it. Example: "Jack be nimble, Jack be quick, Jack jumped over the _____."

★ THE INSTANT CURRICULUM

Pet Stories

3+

Encourages children to develop expressive language.

Words to use

story
favorite
pet
pictures

Materials

paper
pencil
crayons

What to do

1. Ask the children to dictate stories about their favorite pet or about the pet they wish they had.
2. Transcribe the stories onto paper, then let the children illustrate these stories.

★ WHERE IS THUMBKIN?

Magic Pebble

3+

Encourages the development of expressive language.

Words to use

magic
pebble
wish
sentence

Materials

a pebble

What to do

1. Show children a pebble. Tell them you are pretending the pebble is magic and can grant wishes.
2. Let each child hold the pebble and make a wish.
3. Encourage the children to use complete sentences.

★ THE INSTANT CURRICULUM

Can You Remember?

This activity encourages children to sharpen their observati⋯

Words to use

remember
memory

Materials

What to do

1. Ask the children to close their eyes and ask them questions such as: "What color is the bathroom door?" "What did we tape on the window yesterday?"
2. Adapt this activity to different holidays by asking: "What are the names of the things we have on the Christmas tree?" (ornaments, popcorn string, icicles, etc.) "How many bunnies are on the bulletin board?"

★ THE INSTANT CURRICULUM

Thanksgiving Dinner Menu   3+

Children learn memory skills and develop their vocabulary.

Words to use

Thanksgiving
menu
food
special
favorite

Materials

paper
pencil
crayons

What to do

1. Ask the children to describe their Thanksgiving menus. Transcribe what they say onto drawing paper.
2. Then, the children illustrate their dictated menus.

★ WHERE IS THUMBKIN?

Mystery Person

4+

The connection between written and spoken language is reinforced by this activity, as is children's self-esteem.

Words to use

mystery
clue
guess

Materials

large chart paper
markers

What to do

1. When the children are sitting down, take the marker and write "Mystery Person" at the top of the chart.
2. Write and draw clues about a special person in the class.
3. The children have to play detective to discover who the Mystery Person is.
4. Ask the children to look at you. Write the following clue: My eyes are (color).
5. Use pictures and the appropriate color markers to illustrate the clues. For example, use blue to draw blue eyes, brown to draw brown hair, etc.
6. Ask the children to "read" the clue. Point to each word. Next, write the second clue: My hair is (color).
7. Again, read the clue together. Continue writing and reading clues about the Mystery Person's favorite food, songs, stories, games, pets, family, etc. Tell the children to smile when they think they know who it is. At the bottom of the chart write "Who am I?"
8. Read over the entire chart, asking the Mystery Person to stand up at the end. (Make the clues fairly obvious and look directly at that person.) The Mystery Person can draw her picture at the bottom of the page and take it home.

Want to do more?

Use a class list and mark off each child when she is the Mystery Person so you don't leave anyone out.

★ TRANSITION TIME

Communication

4+

How many ways can we communicate?

Words to use

talk
communicate
write
body language
signs

Materials

chart tablet paper
marker

What to do

1. Talk about ways we communicate to others, for example, writing, body language, voice, signs, etc.
2. Make a list of all the communication methods the children can think of.

★ WHERE IS THUMBKIN?

Math Activities

Crayon Patterns

3+

Teaches children about patterns.

Words to use

crayons
colors
pattern

Materials

several boxes of crayons

What to do

1. Empty several boxes of crayons onto the table or floor.
2. Encourage the children to create a pattern with the crayons—two red crayons, one purple crayon, two red crayons, etc.

★ The Instant Curriculum

Feather Match

3+

Teaches one-to-one correspondence and color matching.

Words to use

feather
color
match

Materials

manila folder
red, blue, yellow, green, purple and orange construction paper
scissors
glue

What to do

1. Cut two feathers from each sheet of construction paper.
2. Glue one feather of each color inside the manila folder.
3. Ask the children to match the other feathers to those glued in the folder.

★ WHERE IS THUMBKIN?

Comparisons, Big and Small   3+

Children learn to compare attributes of a variety of objects.

Words to use

big	small
long	short
heavy	light
compare	

Materials

yardsticks	small manipulative blocks
ruler	small and large pictures
rock	large hollow blocks
cotton ball	playdough

What to do

1. Ask the children to describe the objects; then have them make comparisons, such as, this is a big building block in comparison to this little or small one. This is a long yardstick in comparison to this shorter ruler. This rock is heavy in comparison to this light cotton ball.
2. With the playdough, have the children make things to compare. One child may make a tall person and the other a short person. Let the children pair up and decide what they want to make. Compare their sculpting.

Teaching tips

Young preschoolers may not be able to work in conjunction with another child but may prefer to make both of the objects. The fat snake and the thin playdough snake, the foot long playdough hot dog and the one almost all eaten are a few examples they may decide to make. Whenever possible, provide just a few ideas to get them started. Often teachers say too much and the children do not get to think on their own.

★ STORY S-T-R-E-T-C-H-E-R-S

Color of the Day

3+

Teaches children how to make a simple graph.

Words to use

color
favorite
most

Materials

six 4-inch squares cut from construction paper in red, orange, yellow, green, blue and purple
small wooden cubes in the six colors

What to do

1. Place the six colored squares on a table. Ask the children to take a cube of their favorite color and place it on the matching square of construction paper.
2. If there is already a cube on their favorite color, then instruct them to put their cube on top of that one, as if to make a tall building.
3. After all the children have participated in this activity, discuss with them which building is the tallest—which has the most cubes. The answer is the "color of the day."

★ THE INSTANT CURRICULUM

Our Favorite Colors Chart

3+

Children learn to construct a simple graph.

Words to use

colors
crayon
select
favorite

Materials

sheet of typing paper
primary and secondary colored crayons

What to do

1. Ask the children to select their favorite color crayon from a box of primary and secondary colors.
2. Ask each child to make a mark on the sheet of typing paper with his or her selected favorite crayon.

3. Another way to do this activity is to ask one child to conduct a poll of the other children. Instruct the pollster to ask each of the other children to pick his or her favorite color from the crayon box. After each selection, the pollster returns to the table to indicate the child's choice by making a mark on a sheet of paper with the chosen crayon. Continue until all the children have been asked for their favorite color.
4. Now have the pollster look at the sheet of paper and count the number of marks for each color. The teacher can write the totals in the color of crayon. For instance, if five children select red, then write the numeral 5 with the red crayon. Announce the favorite color of most of the children.

Teaching tips

Extend the activity by making a simple graph of the results, an enlarged poster of the typing paper tally.

★ Story S-t-r-e-t-c-h-e-r-s

Measurements   4+

Teaches fine motor development and size concepts.

Words to use

mountain
measure
ruler

Materials

modeling clay or playdough
ruler

What to do

1. Provide the children with playdough or modeling clay.
2. Suggest that they make a mountain.
3. Compare the sizes of the mountains by measuring with a ruler.
4. Think of other ways to measure the mountains.

★ Where Is Thumbkin?

Weighing Seeds

4+

Children learn to use the balance to determine which seeds weigh the most.

Words to use

balance
seeds
observe
heavier

Materials

balance
small plastic covered
    containers
measuring cups
seed corn
bean seeds
pea seeds
sunflower seeds

What to do

1. Demonstrate how to use the balance by having someone pour a cup of corn seed in one side and a cup of bean seeds in the other. Show the children how to tell which weighs more. The side that is lower indicates it is heavier.
2. Have the children make other comparisons and decide which seeds weigh the most.
3. Ask them questions and then write down their observations. For example, "Joey, which seeds did you weigh and which ones weighed more?" Write their answers on index cards. As other children weigh seeds, you can have them investigate and find out if they get the same answer as Joey.

Teaching tips

It is easier to make gross comparisons than to make finer ones. For example, the children can easily see that sixteen peach seeds would weigh more than sixteen bean seeds. For younger children, try these more obvious distinctions.
(Adapted from Linda Larmon Ragsdale's classroom.)

★ Story S-t-r-e-t-c-h-e-r-s

NOVEMBER

math activities

224

How Much Will Our Suitcase Hold?

4+

Children learn to judge capacity.

Words to use

suitcase
pack
clothes
How much will it hold?

Materials

variety of suitcases, duffel bags, backpacks, clothes from the housekeeping and dress-up corner
paper and pencil or pen

What to do

1. Talk about when you pack to go on a trip. It is difficult to decide what to take and what to leave at home, so you look at your suitcase and try to think of all you would like to take.
2. Bring out a suitcase that has clothes hanging out of it and will not close.
3. Take the pieces of clothing out one at a time, and make a list of everything that is in the bag.
4. Bring out a small suitcase and ask the children to guess how much of the clothing from the big bag will fit into the little bag.
5. Let a child or two gather up in their arms the amount of clothing they think will fit and have them pack it in the bag.
6. Continue letting children use different suitcases, duffel bags and backpacks.

Teaching tips

For younger children, simply give them each a suitcase or bag and have them pack it full of clothes, then bring it to you and let them count what they packed. For older children, let them plan what they would need for a trip to different places, then decide which bag fits their needs.

★ More Story S-t-r-e-t-c-h-e-r-s

Hands Up

Children begin to learn the value of numbers with this activity.

Words to use

numeral
envelope

Materials

construction paper
markers
scissors
envelopes

What to do

1. Cut the construction paper into three inch squares. Each child needs five squares.
2. Print the numerals 1-5 on the squares, one on each square. Print an equal number of dots on each card. For example, the number 1 card has one dot on it, the number 2 card has two dots on it, etc.
3. Put a set of numeral cards in each envelope.
4. The children sit on the floor or at tables. Give each child an envelope. Tell the children to spread the cards out in front of them.
5. Call out a numeral. The children find the numeral and hold it up. (With a sweep of your eyes, you can tell who has grasped each concept.)
6. With older children, clap your hands and ask the children to hold up a card to represent the number of claps.

Want to do more?

With younger children, use three numbers. Give older children the numerals 1-10 or higher. Make Hands Up cards using shapes, colors or letters.

★ TRANSITION TIME

NOVEMBER

math activities

Piggy Banks

Teaches children about the monetary value of pennies.

Words to use

bank
penny
How many...?

Materials

ten baby food jars
some pennies

What to do

1. Punch slots in the lids of the baby food jars. Write the numbers one through ten on the jars.
2. Give the children some pennies and have them drop the appropriate number into each "piggy bank."
3. Questions to ask:
   ✓ How many pennies will you put into this bank?
   ✓ Could you put the banks in order from one to ten?
   ✓ If you wanted to buy a piece of penny bubble gum, which bank would you get the money out of?
   ✓ If I wanted you to give me six cents from two banks, which two would you choose to use? How about eight cents?

Show me a bank that has the same number of pennies as your age.
Count all the pennies and tell me how many there are.

★ THE INSTANT CURRICULUM

NOVEMBER

math activities

Music and Movement Activities

Do You Hear What I Hear? 3+

Children have to listen carefully to sounds in this activity.

Words to use

instrument
rhythm
sounds like

Materials

rhythm band instruments

What to do

1. Group the children in a circle.
2. Place three rhythm band instruments in the center of the circle.
3. While the other children have their eyes closed, one child sounds the instruments in an order of her choice.
4. Another child is selected to repeat the order of sounds.
5. To increase the level of difficulty, increase the number of instruments.

★ THE INSTANT CURRICULUM

The Bear Went over the Mountain 3+

Sing this song while waiting for an activity to begin. Children practice sequencing and language skills as they sing along.

Words to use

bear
mountain
over
brownies

Materials

What to do

1. This song is a fun twist on an old favorite.

The bear went over the mountain.
The bear went over the mountain.
The bear went over the mountain.
And what do you think he saw?

He saw a plate of brownies.
He saw a plate of brownies.
He saw a plate of brownies.
And what do you think he did?

He ate up all the brownies, etc. ...
He got a tummy ache, etc. ...
He took some Alka Seltzer, etc. ...
He went and told his mommy, etc. ...
She sent him to his room, etc. ...

He never went over the mountain.
He never went over the mountain.
He never went over the mountain.
To see what he could see.

Want to do more?

Make a big book for this song, letting two or three children illustrate each verse. Use poster board or large grocery sacks for the pages. Do a language experience chart based on this song. Let each child dictate a sentence about what she thinks the bear saw on the other side of the mountain.

★ Transition Time

Button, Button, Who Has the Button?   3+

Children learn to follow the simple rules of a game.

Words to use

button   music
behind   back
drop

Materials

a large button
recording of lively music
tape or record player

What to do

1. Have the children sit in a circle.
2. Explain the rules of "Button, Button, Who Has the Button?" When the music starts, everyone puts their hands behind their backs, making cups for the button.
3. The child who is "it" moves around the circle pretending to drop the button in each hand. The child drops the button in someone's hand and then keeps pretending to drop it until the music stops.
4. When the music stops the teacher chooses a child who guesses who might have the button by saying, "Button, button, who has the button? I think Brian has the button."
5. It doesn't matter if the person guesses incorrectly, whoever has the button holds it up and says, "Button, button, I have the button." The person with the button becomes "it."
6. Demonstrate the game once by being "it." Then, begin the game with one of the children.

Teaching tips

The teacher can usually tell who has the button by the expression on the child's face. By controlling when the music stops and who guesses, the teacher can be certain that all children participate.

★ Story S-t-r-e-t-c-h-e-r-s

Friendship Song   3+

Children learn to sing a short song about friendship.

Words to use

friend
meet
together
play

Materials

What to do

1. Sing this friendship song to the tune of "Here We Go Round the Mulberry Bush."

> *Today, I'm going to meet a friend, meet a friend, meet a friend.*
> *Today, I'm going to meet a friend and we'll be friends together.*
>
> *Today, I'm going to play with my friend, play with my friend, play with my friend.*
> *Today, I'm going to play with my friend and we'll be friends forever.*
> *By Shirley Raines*

2. Arrange the children into pairs of friends for the motions of the song.

3. When the song says, "Today," turn hands over with palms up, then the child points to herself for "I," waves "hi" back and forth for the "meet a friend" phrase and ends with two fingers held up for the "together" phrase. Repeat the "Today" and "I" motions for the second verse, then wave arms as if calling someone over for the "play with my friend" phrase. End by hugging oneself for the "friends forever"
4. Sing the song (with or without hand motions) at several transition times throughout the day, including while cleaning up the room.

Teaching tips

Teachers often feel inhibited about singing. To get over those inhibitions, learn a few songs to sing with a record or cassette tape, then simply burst into song whenever you feel like singing. Or hum the tune and let the children guess what it is. It is amazing how a few good songs can brighten a rainy day or calm the most rambunctious child.

★ Story S-t-r-e-t-c-h-e-r-s

Doing the Turkey Trot   3+

Children learn to move as the lyrics direct them.

Words to use

left   right

Materials

Arthur's Thanksgiving by Marc Brown

What to do

1. Teach the children to do the "Hokey Pokey."
2. Write new lyrics to the "Hokey Pokey" using the names of the turkey body parts instead of the children's body parts. For example, when the song says, "Put your right arm in," let the children sing

> *You put your right wing in,*
> *You put your right wing out,*
> *Put your right wing in*
> *And flutter it all about.*
> *You do the turkey trot and*
> *You turn yourself around.*
> *That's what it's all about.*
>
> By Shirley Raines

3. Continue adding verses for the long neck to stretch it all about, spreading tail to strut it all about and beak to gobble it all about.
4. Read *Arthur's Thanksgiving*. Then, rehearse the song and sing it and do the motions for another class as your version of Arthur's Thanksgiving Play.

Teaching tips

Young children do not do well with scripted plays. If your children are invited to perform for a school function, have them sing or do movement activities that they already know.

★ More Story S-t-r-e-t-c-h-e-r-s

Pots and Pans for Our Kitchen Band

Children learn to march and keep the beat on their kitchen utensils and pots and pans.

Words to use

box
pots
pans
lids
march
band

Materials

large cardboard box
pots and pans, lids, coffee
  cans
large metal and wooden
  serving spoons, table-
  spoons
cassette recording of
  march music
tape player

What to do

1. Collect all the instruments, pots, pans and utensils for the kitchen band and place them in a large cardboard box.
2. Play some march music and let the children parade around the edge of the circle time rug, marching and clapping their hands.
3. The children sit down. Randomly call out the names of children to come up and select an instrument for the kitchen band.
4. March around the room, leading the kitchen band as they keep time with the march music.

Teaching tips

Banging around on pots and pans and coffee cans certainly is not real music; however, the improvised pretend band can enjoy the movement of the activity.

★ MORE STORY S-T-R-E-T-C-H-E-R-S

Musical Instruments

Children learn to identify instruments and their sounds.

Words to use

instrument
play
music
mandolin
violin
harmonica
flute
drum
accordion

Materials

as many as possible of the following instruments and musicians who play them: mandolin, harmonica, flute, drum, violin, accordion
cassette tapes and recorder

What to do

1. Invite adults or older children who can play these instruments to come to class and bring their instruments with them. Invite one musician per day, and when all the musicians have visited, ask them to come together on one day and play together.
2. Have the musician play a song he likes and then play a song the children might know, such as "Twinkle, Twinkle, Little Star." Record the songs on cassette tape.
3. After the musicians have played, let the children hold and play the instruments, following the instructions the musician gives.

Teaching tips

Contact a music teacher or a band leader and ask to have older children bring their band instruments and play for the class.

★ More Story S-t-r-e-t-c-h-e-r-s

Science Activities

Feed the Critters

3+

Birds, squirrels and other animals live in every backyard and playground, coming and going in their own daily rhythm. Providing a reliable food source allows these critters to be observed daily and recognized as a consistent part of the environment.

Words to use

observe
record
identify
time

Materials

water dish
grains
dry cereals
all types of seeds
cracker crumbs
raw vegetables, etc.
recording materials, i.e. pencil, paper, tape recorder

What to do

1. Place a variety of foods out on the playground or in the backyard.
2. Keep an eye open for the different kinds of critters that come to eat.
3. Record on paper or on the tape recorder the children's comments about the different critters and the foods they prefer.
4. Record the times that different critters come to eat.

Want to do more?

Make a graph depicting kinds of animals, frequency of visits and food preferred. Try placing the food out overnight. Move the food source to various parts of the yard. Do you think you are meeting the food needs of all animals that might visit? You might consider a hummingbird feeder or thistle seed for the goldfinches.

★ HUG A TREE

Newspaper Construction

Children love to build things they can play in. Instead of expensive hollow blocks, roll newspapers into logs for life-size construction. Children build with them for hours, experience balance, cause and effect, structure strength, angles, curves and shapes. You'll be impressed with what you see.

Words to use

build
construct
shape
angle
strength
architect
plan
site

Materials

newspaper
tape

What to do

1. Take two sheets of newspaper and roll into a tight roll. Tape with masking tape to prevent unrolling—a small piece or two is all that is needed. The completed roll is 1 to 3 inches in diameter. Let the children help.
2. Repeat the above procedure until you have 50 to 500 newspaper logs. (Believe us—this doesn't take as long as you think!)
3. Let the children construct anything they want—a tower, a house, a rocket ship, a bus, a train, an igloo, a fence. Some structures will be self-supporting, others will need the help of props or tape.

Want to do more?

Supplement newspaper logs with other building materials to create new and interesting constructions. Open sheets of newspaper, blankets, chairs, card tables and coffee tables can provide materials for expanding this activity throughout the room. Let the children play architect. The younger children can talk about plans and ideas as the older ones sketch ideas on paper. Design a house for the guinea pig. Visit a construction site. Discuss blueprints to show what grownups do when they are engaged in similar activities. Discuss cause and effect, e.g., Our building keeps falling down! Why? How can we build it so it won't fall down?

★ MUDPIES TO MAGNETS

N O V E M B E R

science activities

Hand Magnet Scavenger Hunt

Children explore and discover what kinds of materials are attracted by a magnet and what kinds are not.

NOVEMBER

Words to use

magnet
attract
repel

Materials

craft sticks
magnetic tape
markers

What to do

1. As an introduction, display several different types of magnets for the children to experiment with. Have a brief discussion about magnets and what they do.
2. Tell the children that today they will create their own magnets to use on a magnetic scavenger hunt.
3. Each child takes a craft stick and decorates it using markers.
4. Give each child a piece of magnetic tape to attach to the back of the decorated craft stick.
5. Take children to the room where they will conduct their magnetic scavenger hunt. Talk about where in the room children can search for items that may or may not be attracted by their magnets.
6. Ask each child to predict an object that she thinks might be attracted by the magnet. Make a list of the children's predictions.
7. Conduct the scavenger hunt.
8. After the scavenger hunt, as a group, go over the prediction list. Ask questions like, "Which of these items were attracted by the magnet?" "What do they have in common?" "What other things did you find on the hunt that were attracted by the magnet?"
9. Make a list of all items found on the scavenger hunt that were attracted by the magnet.

Want to do more?

Send the hand magnets home so children can conduct a scavenger hunt at home and report their findings to the class. Keep a picture journal of items that were attracted by the hand magnet.

Book to read

Mickey's Magnet by Franklin Branley

★ THE GIANT ENCYCLOPEDIA OF THEME ACTIVITIES

science activities

The Main Attraction: Magnet Boxes

Magnet boxes allow children to work freely with iron filings and other materials without mess or worry. Work with magnets can then become an independent activity, available to children at any time.

Words to use

magnets
iron filings
attract
force field (the non-cartoon version)

Materials

a shallow box with a clear plastic lid
    such as a stationery box (or a shallow
    box and heavy plastic wrap)
heavy tape such as duct or book
    binding tape
magnets
iron filings—these are available from
    hardware stores who cut thread on
    iron pipe or from scientific supply
    companies (see your local yellow
    pages)

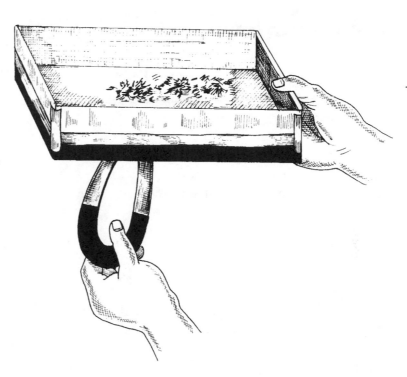

What to do

1. Assemble the magnet boxes with or without the children. Place enough iron filings in the box to barely cover the bottom. Cover with the lid or heavy plastic wrap. Seal the box completely with the tape. While you're at it, reinforce the corners. If you have done all this properly, you will have a sturdy, escape-proof box. You may want to make several, depending on the number of children you have as only one child can use it at a time. Play with it a while to discover for yourself what can be done.
2. Show the children how to use the box by moving a magnet across the bottom to make the iron filings move. They look through the top to see the results. Using the magnet on the plastic side is certainly permissible, the results just aren't as dramatic. The kids will soon discover this on their own.
3. After the children have had a chance to thoroughly explore the possibilities of the magnet boxes, they may begin to talk about the pattern created when the magnet is first touched to the bottom of the box. If not, show them. Different magnets produce different designs. Demonstrate with an assortment if possible. Tell the children that this is one type of real force field. It shows that area that is affected by the power of the magnet. Some magnets are more powerful than others and so affect a larger area. If you like, you can make permanent magnet pictures. Use the time tested method of sprinkling filings on sturdy paper, placing the magnet underneath, and spraying the resulting design with clear varnish.
4. The magnet boxes should be available to the children so that the fun and experimentation can continue over an extended period of time. Big ideas need time to be absorbed. The boxes make it easy to give the children that valuable time.

Want to do more?

Vary the amount of iron filings in the boxes. Place other objects in the boxes with or without the filings. You might want to use some things that magnets don't attract.

★ MUDPIES TO MAGNETS

Rainbow Stew   3+

Rainbow stew, a squeezable mixture in a sealed bag, allows children to play with color mixing and squoosh as much as they like—all with no mess!

Words to use

color names	mix
blend	combine
change	knead

Materials

cornstarch	sugar
mixing bowl	measuring cups
heat source	pan
duct tape	heavy duty sealable bags
red, yellow and blue food coloring	

What to do

1. Prepare the following mixture:
   > Mix 1/3 cup sugar and 1 cup cornstarch.
   > Add 4 cups cold water.
   > Pour into a pan and heat until it begins to thicken, stirring constantly.
   > Cool.
2. Divide the mixture into 3 equal parts. Put each part in a separate container, then add food coloring—one color per container—until the mixtures reach the color intensity desired.
3. Add 3 heaping tablespoons full of each color to a heavy duty sealable bag.
4. Seal the bag and tape it closed. Label each bag with a child's name.
5. Have the children knead their bag, mixing the colors into a rainbow stew.
6. Hang the finished rainbow stew on a wire stretched over the window so everyone can enjoy the creations.

Want to do more?

Putting different amounts of colored mixtures in the bag varies the colors created. Heat or cool the mixtures and observe the differences. In time, these mixtures may get moldy, so store them in the refrigerator.

★ MUDPIES TO MAGNETS

Monthly Guessing Jar

This activity develops math skills through estimating, graphing and counting.

Words to use

jar
objects
estimate
guess

Materials

jar or container
objects to put in the jar (erasers, candy, cotton balls, etc.)
bar graph with each child's name printed on it

What to do

1. Fill the jar with objects and display on your desk.
2. Hang graph on the blackboard.
3. Discuss estimating and graphing with the children.
4. Let children fill in the bar graph using crayon or marker during free time to estimate how many items are in the jar.
5. When all children have had a chance to estimate, empty the jar and count the objects with the children.
6. Divide the counted objects among the children and let them keep them.
7. Those who came closest can get an extra prize from the jar.

★ THE GIANT ENCYCLOPEDIA OF THEME ACTIVITIES

Let's Make Predictions

Children estimate length, width and volume and extend their vocabulary to include the words: feet, yards, inches, pounds and cups.

Words to use

feet
yard
inch
pound
cup

NOVEMBER

science activities

Materials

chart paper, large construction paper or poster board
markers
yarn
apple
orange
test tube, small beaker or any other appropriate containers
small chips for voting
balance scale
clear plastic measuring cups

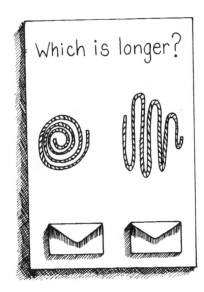

What to do

1. On the first day, make the following chart (see illustration) which compares the length of drawings. Use yarn and have children vote by placing one chip in the envelope of their choice. Use identical lengths of yarn to measure the drawings before counting votes.
2. On the second day, have a real apple and orange for the children to see but not hold. Have children guess which is heavier and weigh with a balance scale. Count the votes.
3. On the third day, show a pair of containers (perhaps a test tube and beaker), filled with water and have children vote on which holds more water. Pour water from each container into the same size clear plastic cups to measure. Count the votes.

Want to do more?

Have children measure each other and objects in the room with lengths of yarn. Use the balance scale to compare weights of things like small plastic eggs, blocks or corn.

★ THE GIANT ENCYCLOPEDIA OF THEME ACTIVITIES

Magnet Testing

This activity allows children to make guesses about and test a magnet's strength. They will also compare the relative strength of different magnets.

Words to use

strong
weak
small
large
strength

Materials

magnets of various sizes and types (bar, horseshoe, ring, rod, cylinder, etc.)
large paper clips
small paper clips
chart for recording estimated and actual strengths of each magnet

What to do

1. Unbend one of the large paper clips and place it against the side of one of the magnets.
2. Have the children guess how many paper clips the magnet can hold. Draw a picture of the magnet on the chart and record the guess next to it.
3. One at a time, hang small paper clips on the large one until the large paper clip falls off. The strength of the magnet can be measured by the number of paper clips held before they fall off. Record the actual number on the chart and compare it to the guess.
4. Repeat the process with each magnet.
5. Answer the following questions:
   ✓ Is one type of magnet consistently stronger than the others?
   ✓ Is the strength of a magnet related to its size?
   ✓ Are magnets strongest at their ends?

Want to do more?

Make available a basket with different items that the children can sort into two groups—those that are attracted to the magnet and those that are not. Experiment with the strength and pulling power of magnets using assorted materials.

Books to read

Adventures in Physical Science by Margy Kuntz
Science with Magnets by Helen Edom
The Science Book of Magnets by Neil Ardly

★ THE GIANT ENCYCLOPEDIA OF THEME ACTIVITIES

NOVEMBER

science activities

Magnet, Yes or No?

4+

This activity will help children to draw conclusions about the kind of objects that a magnet will attract.

Words to use

magnet
attract
predict
experiment
sort
metal

Materials

large horseshoe or bar magnet
items to be tested with the magnet (e.g. bottle cap, rubber band, leaf, feather, paper clip, ring or earring, coin, piece of yarn, nail file, little metal car, block, sand, slice of bread)

What to do

1. Display all items, including the magnets, on a table.
2. Ask the children what they already know about magnets. Listen for any misconceptions they might have, but don't correct them.
3. Ask the children to predict what items can be picked up by the magnet.
4. Allow them to experiment—either individually or as a group—with the magnet and the items on the table.
5. As the children experiment, sort the items into two piles—those that attract the magnet and those that do not.
6. Lead a discussion afterwards about what the objects that attracted the magnet have in common. Reinforce the idea that metal objects attract the magnet.

Want to do more?

Divide a bulletin board in half and show things a magnet will attract and things it will not attract. Label the bulletin board with a picture of a magnet. Mark each half with a plus sign (for will attract) and a minus sign (for will not attract). Invite the children to bring objects to test with the magnet. Items can be taped, strung, glued, tacked or stapled to the appropriate side of the bulletin board.

Book to read

Amazing Magnets by David Adler

★ THE GIANT ENCYCLOPEDIA OF THEME ACTIVITIES

Who Am I?

Encourages observation skills and critical thinking.

Words to use

animal
questions
identify

Materials

one-half sheet of poster
    board
laminated animal and pet
    pictures
Velcro
scissors

What to do

1. Cut a small circle (the size of a child's face) on one-half of the poster board.
2. Glue a Velcro strip on the other half of the poster board and on the back of each of the animal pictures.
3. One child holds up the board and places her face through the hole.
4. Without letting the first child see, another child places an animal on the Velcro strip on the board.
5. The child holding the board asks the other children yes/no questions about the animal on the board.
6. Repeat with another child and another animal.

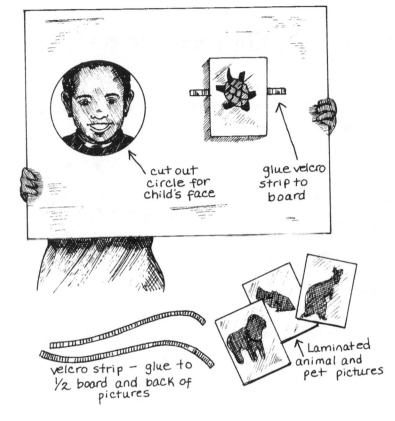

cut out circle for child's face

glue velcro strip to board

velcro strip — glue to ½ board and back of pictures

Laminated animal and pet pictures

★ WHERE IS THUMBKIN?

Snack and Cooking Activities

No-Bake Pumpkin Custard

3+

A yummy way to learn about measurement.

Words to use

pumpkin
measure
pie

Materials

canned pumpkin pie filling
marshmallow creme
whipped topping
cinnamon
mixing bowl and spoon
measuring spoons
bowls and spoons

What to do

1. With the children's help, mix together two tablespoons of pumpkin pie filling, one tablespoon of marshmallow creme and one tablespoon of whipped topping for an individual portion. Place in a serving bowl.
2. Repeat for each child in the class.
3. Sprinkle cinnamon on top.
4. Eat. Yum!

★ WHERE IS THUMBKIN?

Cinnamon Cider Drink

3+

Children learn to prepare a hot drink.

Words to use

warm
cider
mug
cinnamon

Materials

apple cider
hot plate or microwave
large saucepan
mugs
teaspoons
cinnamon stick or can of cinnamon

What to do

1. With a small group of children assisting, pour the apple cider into a large saucepan and heat until it is warm. Use a large glass mixing bowl with spout for microwave.
2. Pour the warm cider into mugs, filling about half full.
3. Let the helpers stir the cider with a cinnamon stick or sprinkle a bit of cinnamon into the mug and stir.
4. Ask your assistants to invite the other children over for warm cinnamon cider.

Teaching tips

Individual packets of apple cider mix can also be used. The water can be warmed in a coffee maker and the children can each mix their own mug of cider. Many families have extra cups and mugs which they may be willing to donate. Whenever possible use real cups and mugs which are heavier and easier for children to handle than Styrofoam ones. Real mugs also cut down on the amount of throw-aways and trash generated—a way your class can help with environmental concerns.

★ More Story S-t-r-e-t-c-h-e-r-s

Celery Crunchies   3+

Children learn how to prepare celery crunch snacks.

Words to use

celery
crunchy
filling
pimento
cream cheese

Materials

two or three stalks of celery
cream cheese or pimento cheese or peanut butter
knives and cutting boards
spreaders
vegetable brush

What to do

1. With the children helping, wash the celery and separate it into stalks.
2. At snack time, each child cuts her own slice from the stalk and fills it with one of the fillings. If possible, include a selection of pimento cheese or peanut butter.
3. Leave at least one stalk whole so that the children can see how it looks when purchased.

Teaching tips

Choose some of the "picky" eaters to help with the snack preparation. They are more likely to try the snack if they are involved in the preparation. Do not force children to eat foods that they dislike, but encourage experimenting. Often young children lack experience with a variety of foods because their families do not serve them or the foods may be prepared differently at home.

★ STORY S-T-R-E-T-C-H-E-R-S

Families Setting the Table and Eating Together   3+

Children pretend to be families during snack time and learn how to set the table.

Words to use

family
set the table
together

Materials

Daddy Makes the Best Spaghetti by Anna Grossnickle Hines
if possible, real silverware, dishes, glassware, napkins and place mats

What to do

1. Look again at the illustration of the family eating together in *Daddy Makes the Best Spaghetti*.
2. Ask the children to sit at the snack tables; then at random ask children to pretend to be the father, mother, grandfather, grandmother and children. At some tables there might not be a mother and at others there might not be a father. Discuss that we are still families even if one of our parents is not present.
3. Have these children sit together as families throughout the week during snack time.
4. Let different "members of the family" take turns setting the table.

Teaching tips

With older children, encourage table conversations with each person maintaining their role. With younger children, since snack time is not usually a pretending time, a teacher, aide or volunteer may need to sit at the table to encourage conversation.

★ MORE STORY S-T-R-E-T-C-H-E-R-S

Crunchy Veggies

Children learn to wash, peel and cut vegetables for a snack.

Words to use

crunchy
vegetable names
peel
pare

Materials

carrots, celery, zucchini, cucumbers, broccoli, vegetable peelers, vegetable brush, paring knives, cutting boards, serving tray, napkins
My Friend Leslie: The Story of a Handicapped Child by Maxine B. Rosenberg

What to do

1. Demonstrate for the cooking and snack helpers how to wash the vegetables, including using the vegetable brush.
2. When they have finished washing the vegetables, demonstrate how to use the vegetable peelers and knives.
3. Peel and cut the vegetables.
4. Let the children arrange the vegetables in a nice arrangement on a serving tray.
5. Read *My Friend Leslie*. Then, serve the vegetables at snack time and discuss how Leslie and Karin liked peeling carrots when their class was preparing a stew.

Teaching tips

Some teachers are reluctant to let young children have real paring knives. If you have the snack helpers sit at a table with you and show them how to place the vegetable down on a cutting board and how to hold the knife, they are quite capable of remembering the safety precautions.

★ MORE STORY S-T-R-E-T-C-H-E-R-S

Transition Activities

Squat and Sit

3+

Sometimes children forget where they are, and this technique will bring them back to reality, help them regain self-control and focus on what they should be doing.

Words to use

squat
sit
stop
whisper

Materials

What to do

1. If children are running around the room and are out of control, call out "Squat and Sit" and wait for them to squat down on the ground or sit on the floor.
2. When the children are still, whisper what you want them to do or go around the room and tap them on the head to signal they may get up and move again.

Want to do more?

On the playground or in the middle of a game, tell children to stop and put their hands on their heads. Call out "1-2-3 Freeze" and wait for the children to freeze in place. Then give them directions. Turn off the lights to calm children down. Change your voice to get children's attention. Make it high and squeaky, then low like a growl.

★ TRANSITION TIME

Setting the Table

The children will learn to set the table with the proper placement of plate, glass, napkin and eating utensils.

Words to use

plate
glass
fork
knife
spoon
space mat

Materials

construction paper
markers
clear contact paper

What to do

1. Make a place-setting pattern with each child by using a permanent marker and drawing around the plate, the base of the glass, the outline of a folded napkin, the outline of a knife, fork and spoon. Draw the pattern onto a plastic place mat or onto construction paper and then laminate the construction paper or cover it with clear contact paper.
2. Provide patterned place mats of the place settings for the housekeeping corner on a permanent basis.
3. Use the place-setting place mats at snack time until the children know the arrangement.
4. Send the patterned place mats home with a note encouraging parents to let their children help set the table at home.

Teaching tips

Practice good manners and proper use of utensils at snack time. Whenever possible, use real silverware instead of throw-away plastics. If plastics are used for snacks, at least place real utensils in the housekeeping center.
(Adapted from Mary Legan's classroom.)

★ Story S-t-r-e-t-c-h-e-r-s

Boom Chica Boom

What a silly way to dramatize and practice language skills!

Words to use

echo
chant
repeat

NOVEMBER

transition activities

Materials

What to do

1. Tell the children this is an echo chant.
2. They repeat each line.

> *I said a boom chica boom. (children repeat)*
> *I said a boom chica boom. (children repeat)*
> *I said a boom chica rocka chica rocka chica boom. (children repeat)*
> *Un, huh. (children repeat)*
> *Oh, yeah. (children repeat)*
> *One more time. (children repeat)*

3. Try one of the following versions.

> *Opera version—Sing the verses using arms and a dramatic voice.*
> *Grumpy version—Put a frown on your face and stomp your feet.*
> *Underwater version—Put your forefinger between your lips and move up and down.*

Want to do more?

End this chant with a silent version. Mouth the words without any sound. Make up your own funny version.

★ TRANSITION TIME

Dr. Knicker Bocker

4+

Get rid of wiggles and squirms with this active chant. Dr. Knicker Bocker helps the children develop large muscles, coordination and sequencing skills.

Words to use

rhyme
chant
slap thighs
snap fingers

Materials

What to do

1. Have the children stand up and begin slapping their thighs and snapping their fingers.
2. When everyone has the rhythm, begin the following chant:

Dr. Knicker Bocker
Knicker Bocker
Number nine.
We can get the rhythm
Most any old time.

Who can get the rhythm
In their hands? Clap, clap. (clap hands twice)
Oh, we can get the rhythm
In our hands. Clap, clap. (clap twice)

Who can get the rhythm
In their feet? Stomp, stomp. (stomp feet twice)
Oh, we can get the rhythm
In our feet. Stomp, stomp.

Who can get the rhythm
In their heads? Ding, dong... (move head from side to side)

Who can get the rhythm
In their hips? Hot dog... (put hands on hips and wiggle)

Who can get the rhythm
In their arms? Whoopee! (raise arms and shout, "whoopee!")

Who can get the rhythm
All over? Clap, clap, (put all the previous motions together)
Stomp, stomp,
Ding dong,
Hot dog,
Whoopee!

Want to do more?

For little ones who can't snap, simply slap thighs and clap hands to the rhythm.

★ Transition Time

Number Please

Number Please reinforces the concept of numerical order.

Words to use

numeral
in order

Materials

poster board or heavy
   paper
scissors
markers

What to do

1. Cut the poster board into 3 inch squares. You will need one for each child.
2. Print a numeral on each card.
3. Give each child a card.
4. Ask, "Who has 1?" That child gets in line followed by 2, 3, 4, etc.
5. Let the first child collect the cards before moving to the next activity.

Want to do more?

Change the shape of the cards for different seasons or themes such as fish, dinosaurs, train cars, butterflies or valentines. Have children count in Spanish, Chinese or other languages as they line up.

★ TRANSITION TIME

NOVEMBER

transition activities

Games

Ears Up

3+

What a fun way to learn coordination!

Words to use

follow   leader
group

Materials

What to do

1. One child is selected as the leader.
2. The leader gives directions to the group but the group follows only those directions preceded by the words "ears up," for example, "Ears up, touch your toes."

Want to do more?

This activity can be altered by inserting a new signal word, such as "blinking eyes," "snapping fingers," etc.

★ THE INSTANT CURRICULUM

Clothes Conversation

3+

Teaches children about the weather.

Words to use

clothing   weather
cold   warm

Materials

What to do

1. Show the children three kinds of clothing, for example, a boot, a heavy jacket and a hat.
2. Show one article of clothing at a time and talk about why people wear it.
3. Ask if they have ever been cold or wet, and what kind of clothing they would have liked to put on.

★ 500 FIVE MINUTE GAMES

Exploring Texture

3+

This game offers an enriching prereading experience while developing children's sensory awareness.

Words to use

texture
describe

Materials

What to do

1. Help the children become aware of textures.
2. Ask them to touch a variety of things in the room and help them describe what they feel.
   ✓ Is the floor cool, hard, smooth?
   ✓ Are your cheeks cold, warm, rough, smooth?
   ✓ Do your elbows feel different from your arms?

★ 500 FIVE MINUTE GAMES

High and Low Game

3+

Teaches children about high and low.

Words to use

wiggle
wave
shake
move

Materials

What to do

1. Ask the children to raise their hands in the air.
2. While their hands are in the air, encourage them to wiggle their fingers, wave their wrists and shake their arms.
3. Ask them to put their arms down and make the same movements that they made with their hands high in the air.
4. Ask the children to sit on the floor with one leg high in the air.
5. Ask them to wave their ankles in the air, wiggle their toes and move their legs back and forth.
6. Ask them to put their legs down and make the same movements that they made with their legs in the air.

★ 500 FIVE MINUTE GAMES

Matching Game

Teaches children matching skills.

Words to use

shoes
pile
matching
pair

Materials

What to do

1. Have the children take off their shoes and place them in a pile.
2. Mix them up to separate the pairs.
3. Give a shoe to one child and ask her to find the matching one.
4. After she has found it, she gives the pair to the owner
5. This game becomes easier as it continues, when there are fewer shoes to sort through, so choose the children who might find this task difficult later on in the game.

Want to do more?

Match other things besides shoes.

★ 500 FIVE MINUTE GAMES

Books

Anna's Secret Friend by Yoriko Tsutsui
Arthur's Thanksgiving by Marc Brown
Autumn Harvest by Alvin Tresselt
Banza by Diane Wolkstein
Catching the Wind by Joanne Ruder
The Cat's Midsummer Jamboree by David Kherdian and Nonny Hogrogian
The Comic Adventures of Old Mother Hubbard by Tomie dePaola
Farmer Goff and His Turkey Sam by Brian Schatell
Follow Me! by Mordicai Gerstein
Gertrude and the Goose Who Forgot by Joanna Galdone
Good Dog, Carl by Alexandra Day
Go Tell Aunt Rhody by Aliki
Harry the Dirty Dog by Gene Zion
It's Thanksgiving by Jack Prelutsky
Oh, What a Thanksgiving! by Steven Kroll
Over the River and Through the Wood by Lydia Maria Child
Petunia by Roger Duvoisin
The Puppy Who Wanted a Boy by Jane Thayer
Two Good Friends by Judy Delton
We Are Best Friends by Aliki
Where Do All the Birds Go? by Tracey Lewis
Whistle for Willie by Ezra Jack Keats
The Year at Maple Hill Farm by Alice Provensen and Martin Provensen

Records, Tapes and CDs

Beall, Pamela Conn and Susan Hagen Nipp. "She'll Be Comin' 'Round the Mountain" from *Wee Sing Sing-Alongs*. Price Stern Sloan, 1990.

Beall, Pamela Conn and Susan Hagen Nipp. "The More We Get Together" from *Wee Sing Sing-Alongs*. Price Stern Sloan, 1990.

Finkelstein, Marc and Carol. *Every Day's a Holiday*. Melody House.

Moore, Thomas. *The Family*. Thomas Moore Records.

Palmer, Hap. *Marching*, Educational Activities.

Palmer, Hap. *Holiday Songs and Rhythms*. Educational Records, 1971.

Scruggs, Joe. "Swing Low Sweet Chariot" from *Deep in the Jungle*. Rabbit Shadow Records, 1987.

Fall Activities
Listed by Source

500 Five Minute Games

September—Imagination; Looking at Leaves; Musical Math
October—A Different Old MacDonald; The Farm; Gift Giving; Moo, Cow, Moo; This Little Cow Eats Grass; The Wizard; What Would You Do?
November—Clothes Conversation; Exploring Texture; High and Low Game; Matching Game

The Complete Learning Center Book

September—Art Center; Art Museum; Designer Clothes; Housekeeping Center; Making Wigs; A Repair Box; Texture Box
October—Block Center; Prop Boxes; Science and Nature Center
November—Bakery/Cooking Center; Chef Hats; Music and Sound Center; Shakers

Earthways

September—Baking Bread; Baking Whole Apples; Drying Apples; Fancy Cutting
October—Baking Pies; Leaf Banners; Leaf Crowns
November—Fall Lanterns; Nature's People; Stringing Necklaces; Wheat Weaving

The GIANT Encyclopedia of Circle Time and Group Activities

September—All About Our Day; Create a Class Tree; Fall Leaves; Get Acquainted Song; Leaf People; Roll That Ball; "Who's Missing"
October—The Animals on the Farm; Counting Pumpkin Seeds; Jack-o-Happy; Musical Hoops; Peekaboo Farm; Sound Effects; Sticky Dancing; Witch's Brew
November—Family Hats; My Family Tree; Sorting Gourds

The GIANT Encyclopedia of Theme Activities

September—Apple Picking; Coins; Composting; Four Seasons Game; Goldilocks and the Three Bears; Leaf Dance; Let's Make a Telephone; Magic Mirrors; Making Imaginary Applesauce; Photo/Name Match-up Game; Pick an Apple—To Learn Your Name; Piggy Bank; Planting Bulbs; Rice Cake Creatures; The Three Little Pigs; Tissue Square Leaves; What Color Is My Apple?
October—Brown Bear Bread; Cinnamon Roll-up; Goat Masks; Leaf Bookmark; Melt the Witch; Papier-mâché Masks; Sewing a Spider's Web; Spider's Web Game; What's Cooking?
November—Hand Magnet Scavenger Hunt; Thanksgiving Handy Turkey; Let's Make Predictions; Magnet Testing; Magnet, Yes or No?; Monthly Guessing Jar

Hug a Tree

September—Curves and Straights; Spy Glass Treasure Hunt: Close-up and Far Away
October—Grow a Sock; Hide and Seek for Critters and Kids; Leaves Don't All Fall the Same Way; Touch Me, Feel Me, Know Me—or Wake Up Your Fingers; A Wood Chip Garden
November—Feed the Critters

The Instant Curriculum

September—Bathtime for Baby; Color House; Eat Your Dinner, Please; Grocery Sack Leaves In the Bag; Inch by Inch; Musical Beanbags; Seed Sorting; String a Story; This and That
October—And One More...; Button to Button; Fishing Line; Guest Spot; More Rhythmic Nursery Rhymes; Musical Clues; My Number Page; On Stage (formerly In the Boat); Paper Patterns; Pass the Pumpkin; Rhyming Time; Rhythmic Nursery Rhymes; Singing Stages
November—Can You Remember?; Color of the Day; Crayon Patterns; Do You Hear What I Hear?; Ears Up; Magic Pebble; Pantomime Stories; Piggy Banks; Rhyme Time; Silly Sentences

The Learning Circle

September—Autumn Breezes
October—The Alphabet Ghost; Autumn Book

More Mudpies to Magnets

September—Spinner Helicopter
October—Hot and Cold: Let's Get Precise; Tornado Tower; What Is Hiding in the Air?

More Story S-t-r-e-t-c-h-e-r-s

September—One Potato, Two Potato, Three Potato, Four
October—Apples and Pumpkins; Little Pumpkin Pies; Sponge Painting with Fall Colors; Writing Animal Rhymes
November—Cinnamon Cider Drink; Crunchy Veggies; Doing the Turkey Trot; Families Setting the Table and Eating Together; Gilberto and the Wind; How Much Will Our Suitcase Hold?; Musical Instruments; Pots and Pans for Our Kitchen Band; Show This Feeling with Your Face

Mudpies to Magnets

October—Beat a Leaf; Leaf Catchers; Outdoor Hunt and Find
November—Newspaper Construction; Rainbow Stew; The Main Attraction: Magnet Boxes

One Potato, Two Potato, Three Potato, Four

September—Hickory, Dickory Dock; Jack Be Nimble; Little Miss Muffet; One, Two, Buckle My Shoe
October—Little Arabella Stiller; This Little Pig
November—Gobble, Gobble, Gobble; Peas Porridge Hot; Sing a Song of Sixpence

The Outside Play and Learning Book

September—Playing with Mud; What Made This Shape?

The Peaceful Classroom

September—Child in the Dell; The Class Gallery; The Magic Pocket
October—Hot Potato Stories; Knock, Knock; Mystery Person; Rescue Chain
November—Emotions Picture File; Feeling Face Masks; Food for the Hungry; Poor Little Sad Eyes

Preschool Art

September—Branch Weaving; Chalky Leaf Spatter; Finger Puppets; Fingerpaint Leaves; Nature Collage
October—Big Spooky House; Nature Garden; Pumpkin Face Mystery; Spider Web; Stocking Mask
November—Cuff Finger Puppets; Easy Store Puppet Stage; Fuzzy Glue Drawing; String Thing

Story S-t-r-e-t-c-h-e-r-s

September—Baby Apple Pies; Blossoms; Counting Seeds; Country Apples; From Seed to Pear; Here We Go 'Round the Apple Tree; Inverted Glass Experiment; Paper Airplanes; Pear Treats; The Pear Tree; Rhyming Words; Riddle Pictures; Sequencing the Seasons
October—Clean-up Time; Cream Cheese and Jelly Sandwiches; Falling Leaves; Pumpkin Bread
November—Button, Button, Who Has the Button?; Celery Crunchies; Comparisons, Big and Little; Friendship Song; My House, Your House; Our Favorite Colors Chart; Setting the Table; The Tiny Seed; Weather Pictures; Weighing Seeds

ThemeStorming

September—Three Bears Porridge
October—Me and My Shadow; Nasty Faces; Slime; Weave-a-Web; What's a Monster Look Like?

Transition Time

September—Glitter Bottles; Helper Can; Kings, Queens and Helpers; Nutkin; Please and Thank You; Something Special for You; Way Up High in the Apple Tree
October—B-I-N-G-O; Howdy Neighbor; I'm So Glad I Came to School; Look Who's Here Today; Looking Through My Window; Table Talk; Talking Stick; Tickets; Wiggle Them
November—The Bear Went over the Mountain; Boom Chica Boom; Dr. Knicker Bocker; Hands Up; Mystery Person; Number Please; Squat and Sit; Yesterday, Today and Tomorrow

Where Is Thumbkin?

September—Body Language; Heads, Shoulders, Knees and Toes; Hokey Pokey; If You're Happy and You Know It; Open, Shut Them; Shakers; Textured Hands and Feet
October—Animal Puppets; Counting Acorns; The Farmer in the Dell; Gray Squirrel; Haystacks; Making Butter; Nut Sort; The Old Gray Mare; Old MacDonald Had a Farm; Pumpkin Seriation
November—Communication; Family Pictures; Feather Match; Five Fat Turkeys Are We; Go Tell Aunt Rhody; A Home for Puppy; Measurements; The More We Get Together; No-Bake Pumpkin Custard; Oh Where, Oh Where Has My Little Dog Gone?; Pet Stories; She'll Be Comin' 'Round the Mountain; Thanksgiving Dinner Menu; Who Am I?

Sample Rebus Chart

Directions for Making Muffins

1. Preheat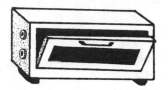

2. Place in

3. Empty  into

4. Add 1  and ½ 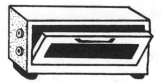 water

5. Stir

6. Pour into

7. Bake in

8. Serve and

Steps in Binding a Book

 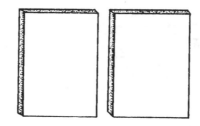 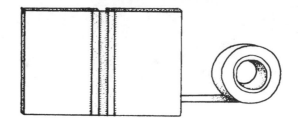

1. Cut two pieces of heavy cardboard slightly larger than the pages of the book.

2. With wide masking tape, tape the two pieces of cardboard together with ½-inch space between.

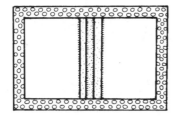  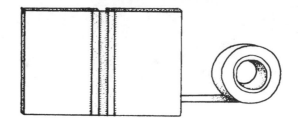

3. Cut outside cover 1½ inches larger than the cardboard and stick to cardboard (use thinned white glue if cover material is not self-adhesive.)

4. Fold corners over first, then the sides.

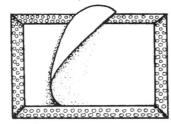 

5. Measure and cut inside cover material and apply as shown.

6. Place stapled pages of the book in the center of the cover. Secure with two strips of inside cover material, one at the front of the book and the other at the back.

Fall
Indexes

Index of Terms

A

acorns, 55, 138
activities, overview of, 11-14
activities, sequencing of, 30
activity, memory strengthening, 93-94
activity for attentive listening, 64
adding machine paper, 137, 154
airplanes, test flights of paper, 72
air pollution, causes of, 161
aluminum cans, 214
aluminum foil, 87
animal pictures, 48, 243
animal puppets, 129
animals
    activities featuring farm, 118-120
    and their food, farm, 174
    hiding places for, 157
apple cider, 245
apple core, 70
apple corers, 79
apple drying process, 83-84
apples, 22, 54, 62, 76-80, 84, 120, 240
apples
    children and, 36
    color identification with, 90-91
    graph of children's favorite, 76
    premixed pie crusts and, 80
    story about, 78-79
    ways of baking, 79

apple snacks, novel cutting of, 76-77
aquarium, 102
artwork, display of children's, 43
attraction of magnets, 242
auditory discrimination skills, 86

B

babies, care of, 40-41
baby food jars, 163, 227
baby tub, 41
backpacks, 225
baking and cooking experiences, 190
baking pan, 79
baking project, unbaked pie shell for, 166-167
balance scale, 102, 224, 240
balloons, 112, 198
balloons for molding starched string, 198-199
banner for fall season, 105-106
bar graph and collected leaves, 154-155
basket, 42, 54, 76, 81, 89, 92, 126, 140, 154, 169
beanbag, 64
beans, 214
bears, 46
behavior, emphasis on acceptable, 208
behavior, responding to children's, 203
bells, 116, 188, 214
belonging, a sense of, 116
belts, 42
binoculars, 65
biscuit cutter, 168
blanket, 38

blindfold, 45, 69, 175
blocks, 221
blocks, benefits from playing with, 100
blossoms, appreciation of, 44
book project, classroom, 121
books as references, time-tested, 11
bouillon, 128
bowls, 46
brainstorming and rhyming, 130-131
branches, 44, 153
bread, 165
bread dough shapes, 163-164
bread from basic ingredients, 81-82
bread tasting, 166
brick, 45
briefcase, 49
bulbs, development of, 71-72
bulletin board, 26, 169
butcher paper, 38
butter, changing whipping cream to, 162-163
butterscotch morsels, 162
buttons, 46, 59, 229

C

cake pan, 151
candles, precautions about, 194
capacities of luggage, 225
cardboard, 40, 74, 87, 93, 111, 139, 145
cardboard box, 27, 232
carrots, 128, 247
catalogs, 30
celery, 128, 245, 247
celery snacks, preparation of, 245-246

Children's Book Index

Recommended Titles

Preschool Art
It's the Process, Not the Product

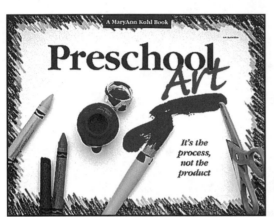

MaryAnn Kohl

Anyone working with preschoolers and early primary age children will want this book. Over 200 activities teach children to explore and understand their world through open-ended art experiences that emphasize the process of art, not the product. The first chapter introduces basic art activities appropriate for all children, while subsequent chapters, which build on the activities in the first chapter, are divided by seasons. With activities that include painting, drawing, collage, sculpture and construction, this is the only art book you will need. 260 pages. © 1994.

ISBN 0-87659-168-3
Gryphon House
16985
Paperback

Mudpies to Magnets
A Preschool Science Curriculum

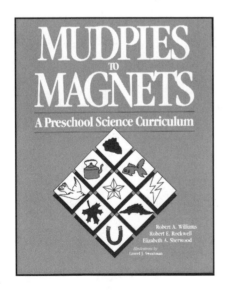

*Elizabeth A. Sherwood, Robert A. Williams,
Robert E. Rockwell*

224 hands-on science experiments and ideas with step-by-step instructions delight and amaze children as they experience nature, the human body, electricity, floating and sinking and more. Children participate in ready-made projects such as making a tornado in a jar, creating constellations and growing crystals. Categorized by curriculum areas, each activity includes a list of vocabulary words. 157 pages. © 1987.

ISBN 0-87659-112-8
Gryphon House
10005
Paperback

**Available at your favorite bookstore,
school supply store or order from Gryphon House®**

Recommended Titles

Cooking Art
Easy Edible Art for Young Children

MaryAnn Kohl and Jean Potter

Children 3-8 years old will enjoy making all of the 150 simple, edible art activities such as Noodle Wreaths, Potato Ghosts, Popcorn Sculpting, and Airplane Cucumbers. Recipes are included for making beverages, sandwiches, desserts, salads, and more. Each recipe allows ample room for cooking artists to explore and create in their own special ways. 191 pages. © 1997.

ISBN 0-87659-184-5
Gryphon House
18237
Paperback

500 Five Minute Games
Quick and Easy Activities for 3-6 Year Olds

Jackie Silberg

Enjoy five-minute fun with the newest book from the author who brought you the popular series Games to Play with Babies, Games to Play With Toddlers, and Games to Play With Two Year Olds. These games are easy, fun, developmentally appropriate, and promote learning in just five spare minutes of the day. Children unwind, get the giggles out, communicate, and build self-esteem as they have fun. Each game indicates the particular skill developed. 270 pages. © 1995.

ISBN 0-87659-172-1
Gryphon House
16455
Paperback

***Available at your favorite bookstore,
school supply store or order from Gryphon House®***

Recommended Titles

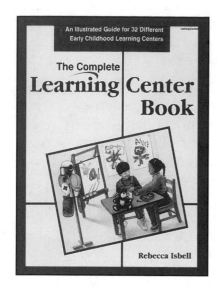

The Complete Learning Center Book
An Illustrated Guide to 32 Different Early Childhood Learning Centers

Rebecca Isbell

Enrich your classroom environment with unique learning centers and new ideas for traditional centers. All you ever needed to know about 32 learning centers is included in this comprehensive book. 365 pages. © 1995.

ISBN 0-87659-174-8
Gryphon House
17584
Paperback

Transition Time
Let's Do Something Different

Jean Feldman

Turn stressful transition times into fun learning experiences with practical, simple activities. from good Morning to Circle Time to Clean-Up, every part of the day is addressed with appropriate, imaginative activities. Periods of time between planned activities will become teachable moments using this invaluable resource. These easy-to-use transition activities will take the teacher smoothly throughout the day, week, month and year. Contains over 400 activities. 288 pages. © 1995.

ISBN 0-87659-173-X
Gryphon House
19844
Paperback

**Available at your favorite bookstore,
school supply store or order from Gryphon House®**